WHY WOULD YOU DO THAT?

BY ANDREA TSURUMI

Hic & Hoc Publications

New Jersey

To Alexander,
goat-leaper of my life.

Why Would You Do That? © 2016 Andrea Tsurumi.
First printing: May 2016.
ISBN: 978-1-68148-102-9.

"Peep of Day" adaptation first published by *At Length*, 2010.
"Food Photographer" first published in *The Brooklyn Rail*, 2012.
"Yup/Nope" first published in *The Brooklyn Rail*, 2014.
"How to Pool" first published in *Quarter Moon* #4 by Locust Moon Press, 2014.
Printed in China
Poodle mustard gas joke courtesy of Alexander Rothman

andreatsurumi.com
hicandhoc.com

TABLE OF CONTENTS

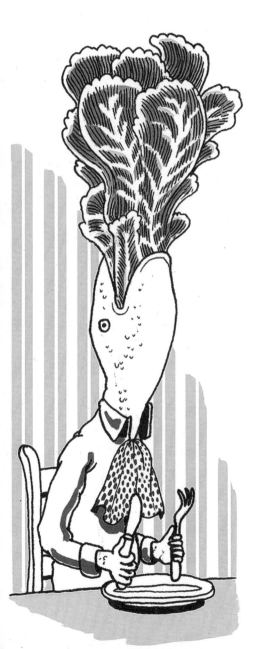

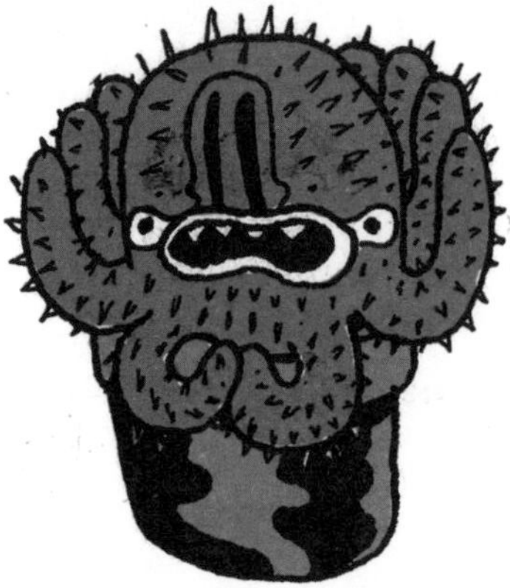
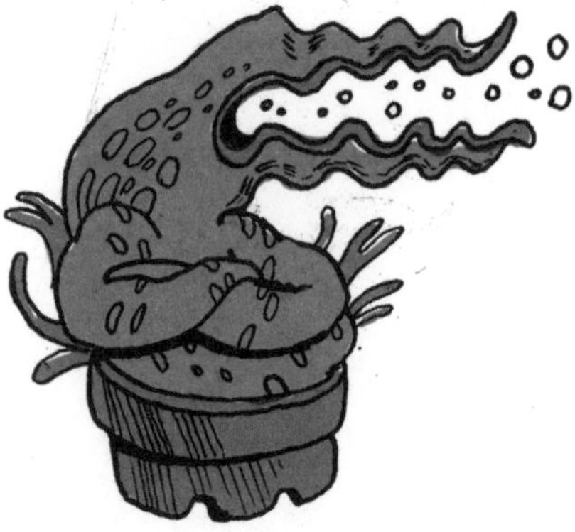
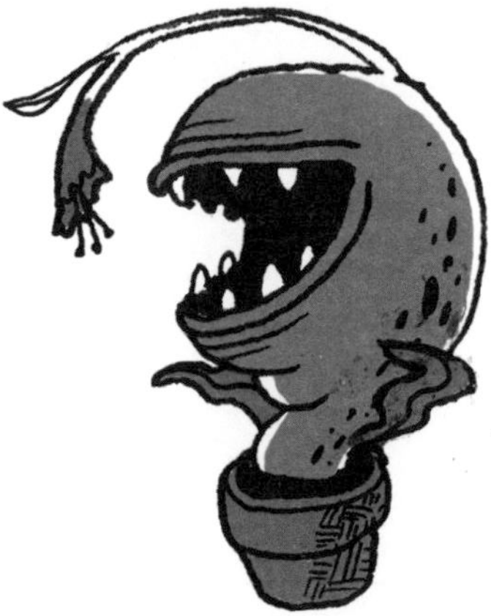
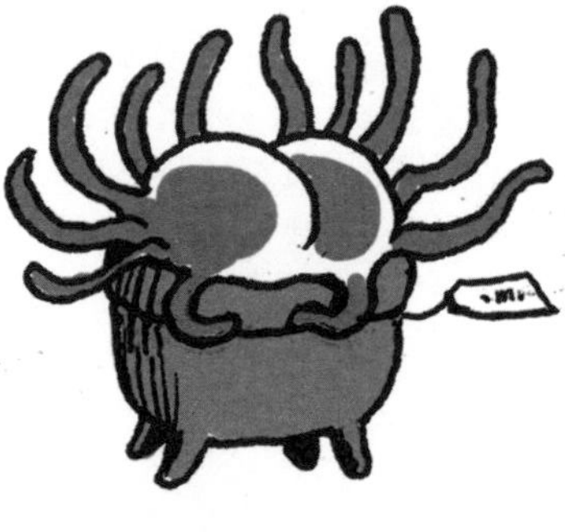
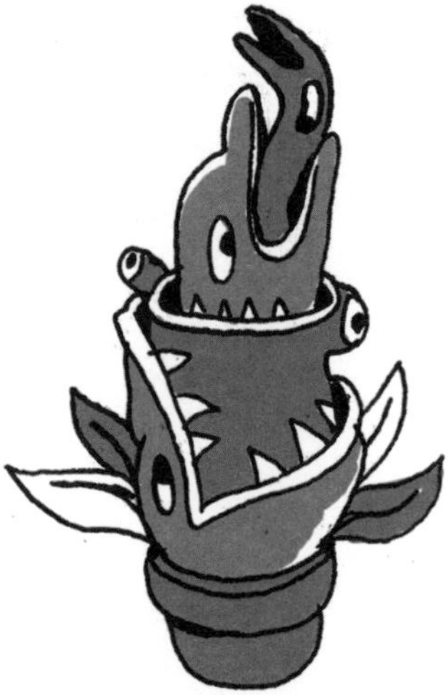
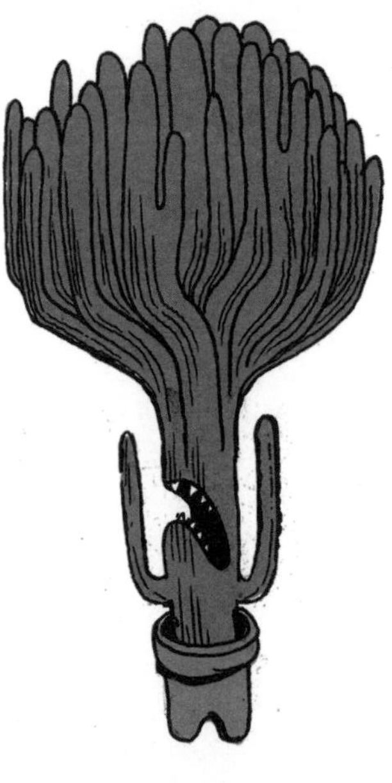

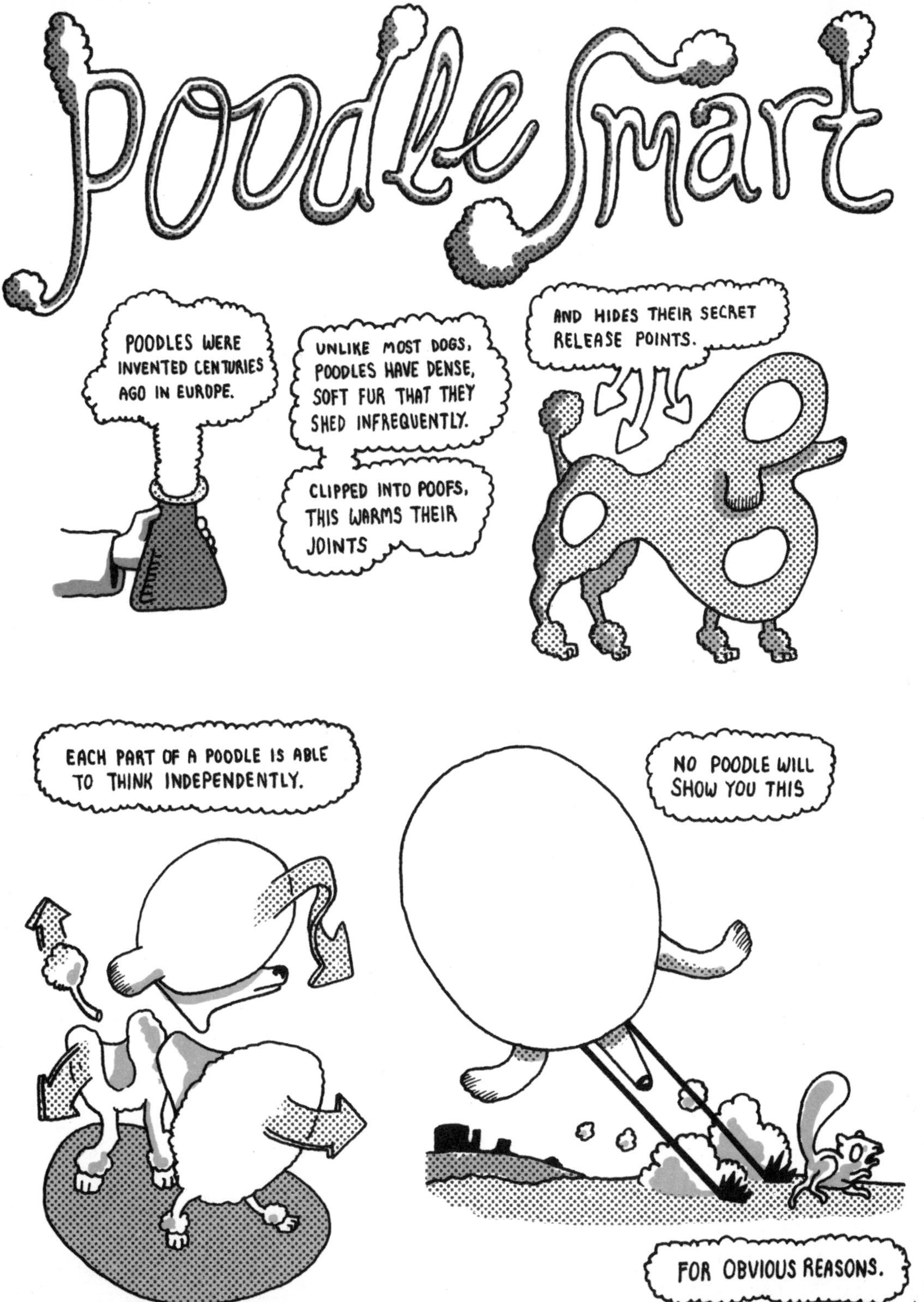
Poodle Smart
POODLES WERE INVENTED CENTURIES AGO IN EUROPE.
UNLIKE MOST DOGS, POODLES HAVE DENSE, SOFT FUR THAT THEY SHED INFREQUENTLY.
CLIPPED INTO POOFS, THIS WARMS THEIR JOINTS
AND HIDES THEIR SECRET RELEASE POINTS.
EACH PART OF A POODLE IS ABLE TO THINK INDEPENDENTLY.
NO POODLE WILL SHOW YOU THIS
FOR OBVIOUS REASONS.

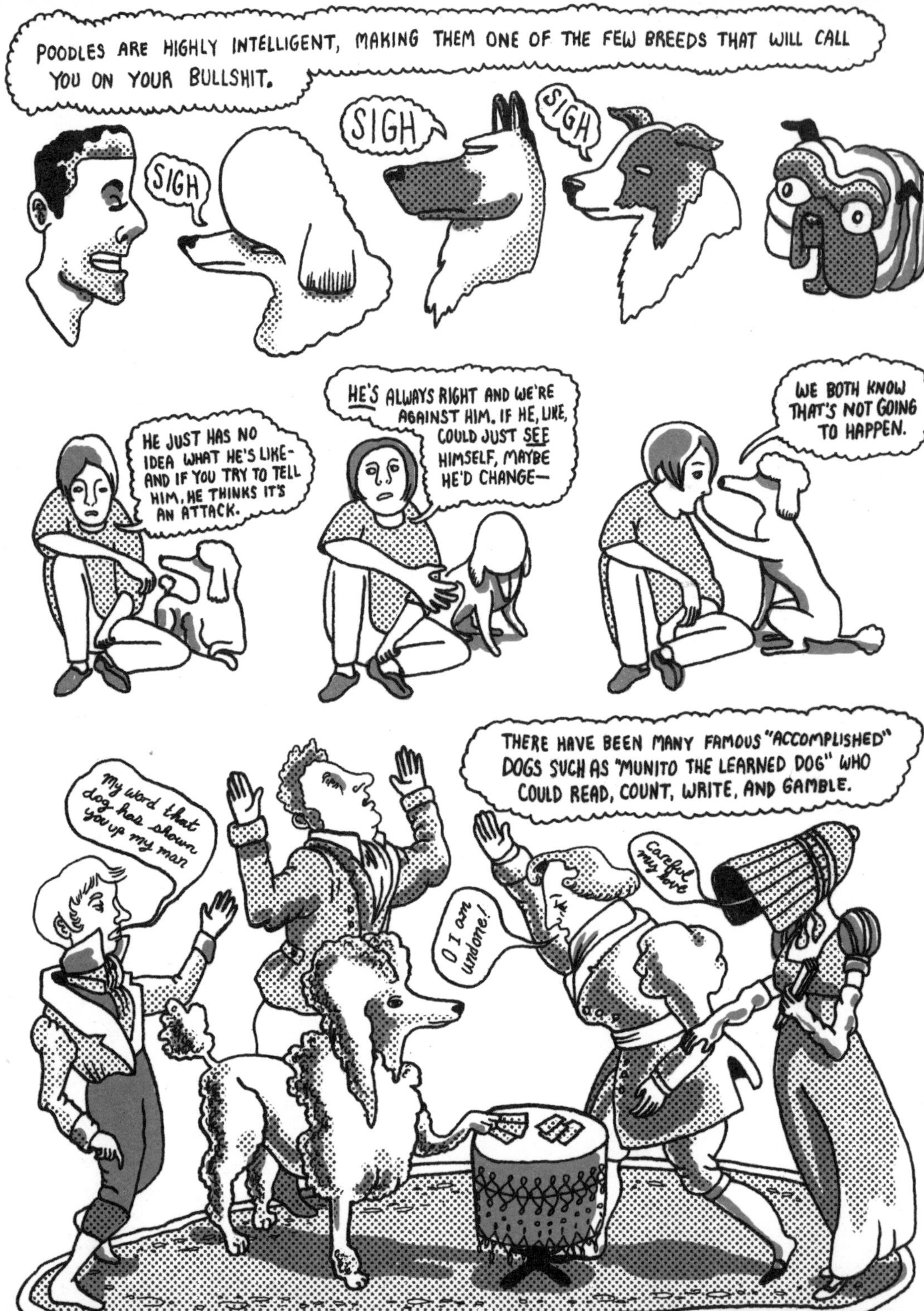
POODLES ARE HIGHLY INTELLIGENT, MAKING THEM ONE OF THE FEW BREEDS THAT WILL CALL YOU ON YOUR BULLSHIT.
SIGH
SIGH
SIGH
HE JUST HAS NO IDEA WHAT HE'S LIKE- AND IF YOU TRY TO TELL HIM, HE THINKS IT'S AN ATTACK.
HE'S ALWAYS RIGHT AND WE'RE AGAINST HIM. IF HE, LIKE, COULD JUST SEE HIMSELF, MAYBE HE'D CHANGE—
WE BOTH KNOW THAT'S NOT GOING TO HAPPEN.
THERE HAVE BEEN MANY FAMOUS "ACCOMPLISHED" DOGS SUCH AS "MUNITO THE LEARNED DOG" WHO COULD READ, COUNT, WRITE, AND GAMBLE.
My word that dog has shown you up my man
O I am undone!
Careful my love

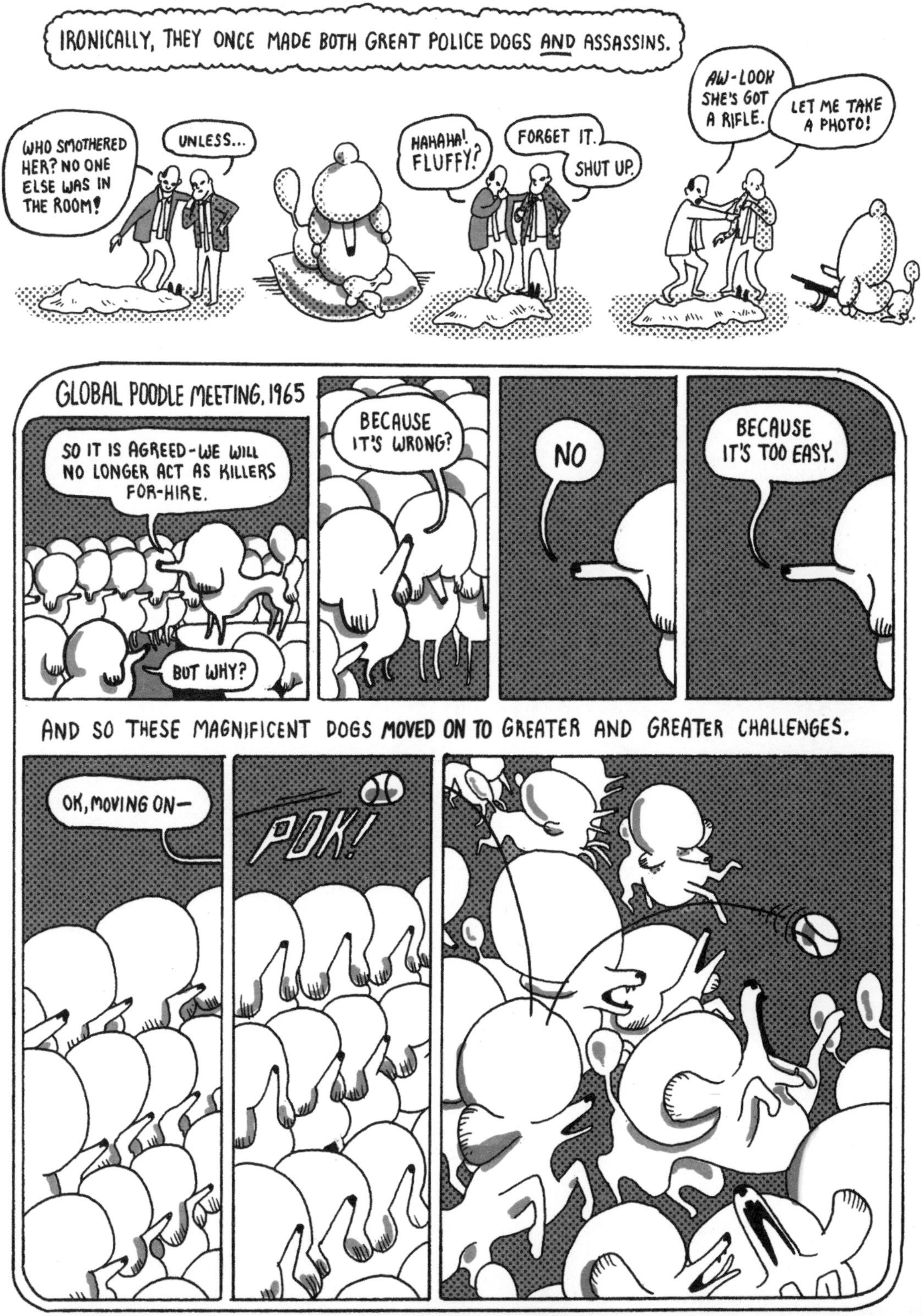
IRONICALLY, THEY ONCE MADE BOTH GREAT POLICE DOGS AND ASSASSINS.
WHO SMOTHERED HER? NO ONE ELSE WAS IN THE ROOM!
UNLESS...
HAHAHA! FLUFFY?
FORGET IT.
SHUT UP.
AW-LOOK SHE'S GOT A RIFLE.
LET ME TAKE A PHOTO!
GLOBAL POODLE MEETING, 1965
SO IT IS AGREED-WE WILL NO LONGER ACT AS KILLERS FOR-HIRE.
BUT WHY?
BECAUSE IT'S WRONG?
NO
BECAUSE IT'S TOO EASY.
AND SO THESE MAGNIFICENT DOGS MOVED ON TO GREATER AND GREATER CHALLENGES.
OK, MOVING ON—
POK!

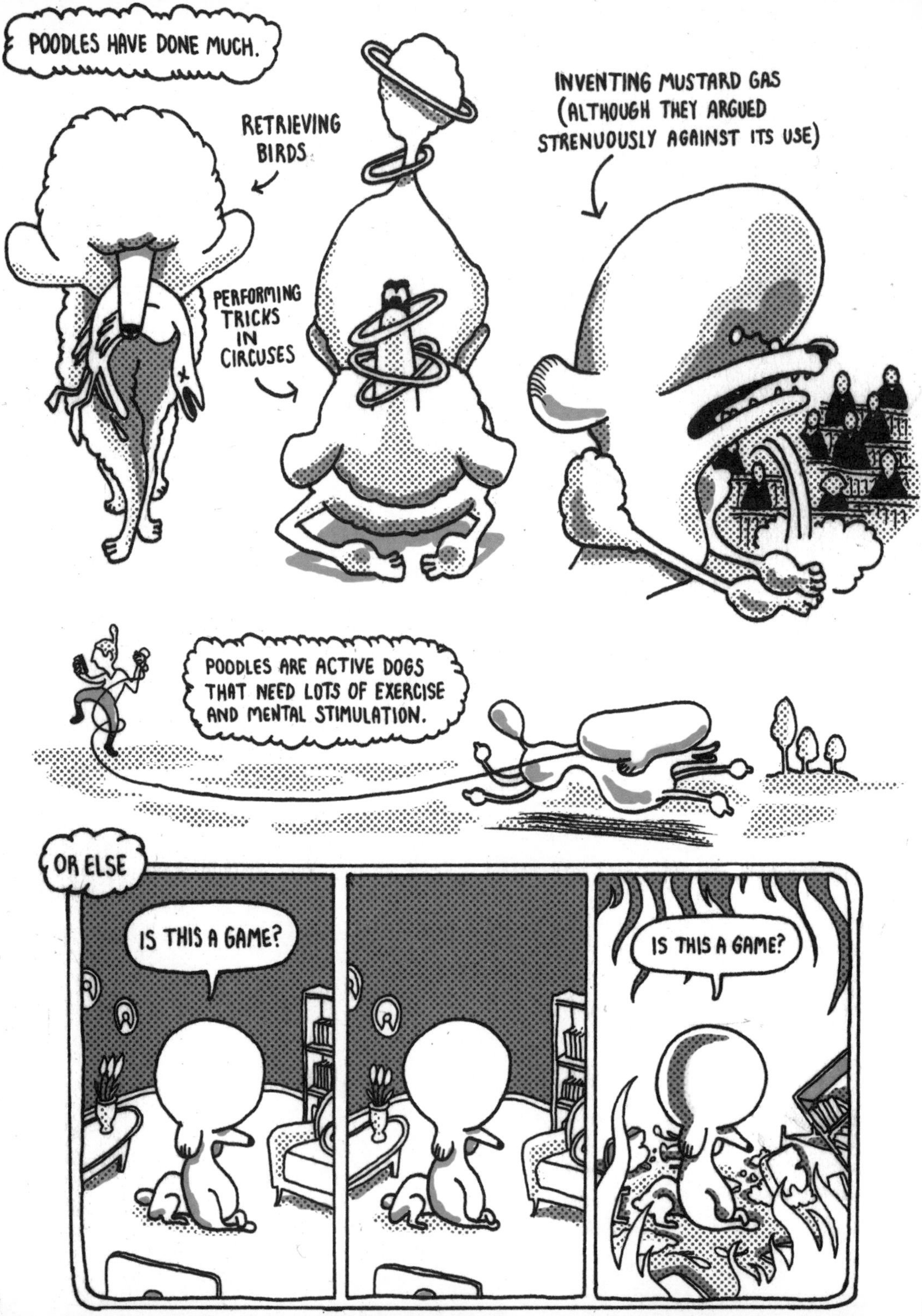
POODLES HAVE DONE MUCH.
RETRIEVING BIRDS
PERFORMING TRICKS IN CIRCUSES
INVENTING MUSTARD GAS (ALTHOUGH THEY ARGUED STRENUOUSLY AGAINST ITS USE)
POODLES ARE ACTIVE DOGS THAT NEED LOTS OF EXERCISE AND MENTAL STIMULATION.
OR ELSE
IS THIS A GAME?
IS THIS A GAME?

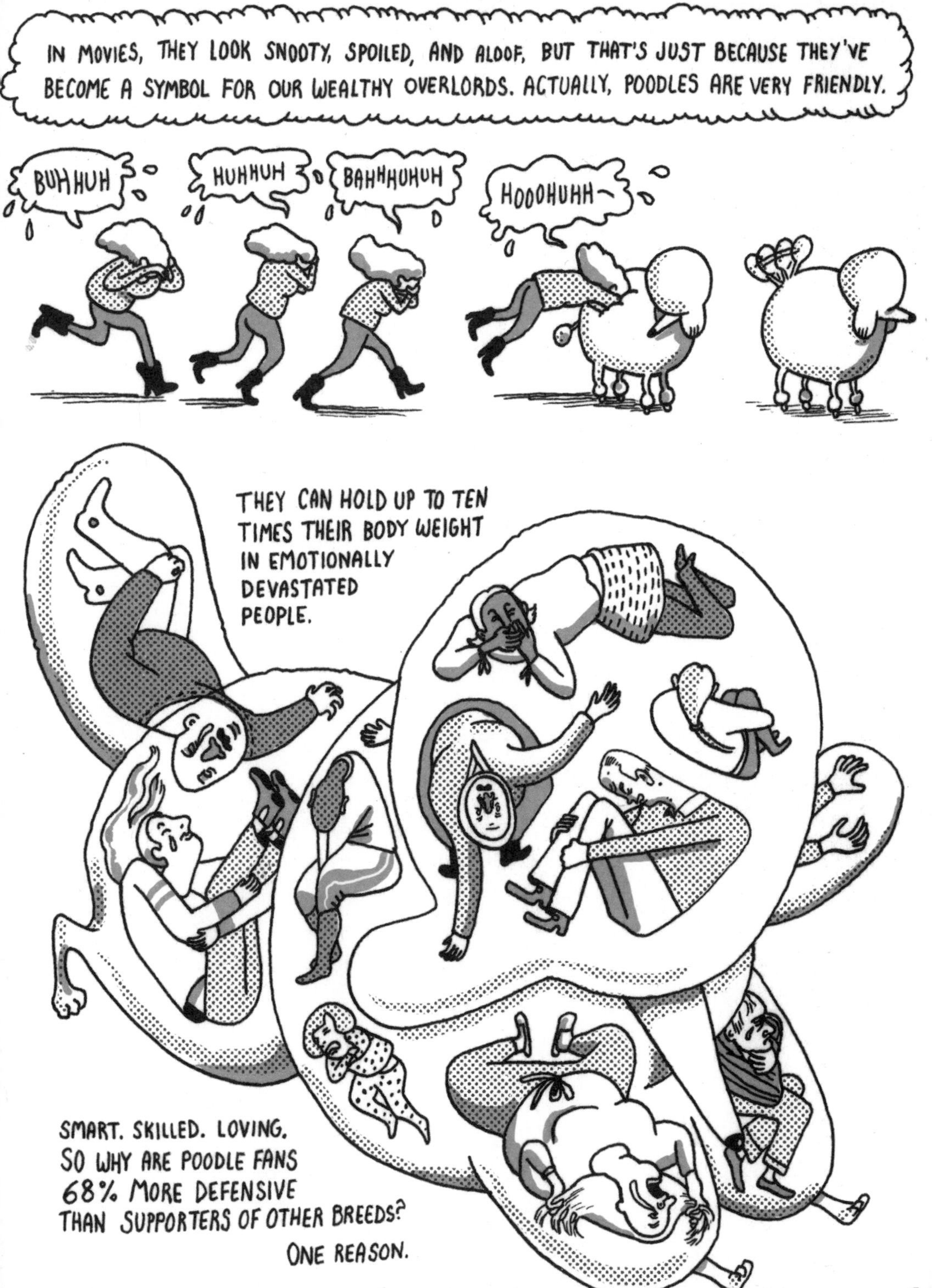

IN MOVIES, THEY LOOK SNOOTY, SPOILED, AND ALOOF, BUT THAT'S JUST BECAUSE THEY'VE BECOME A SYMBOL FOR OUR WEALTHY OVERLORDS. ACTUALLY, POODLES ARE VERY FRIENDLY.
BUHHUH
HUHHUH
BAHHHUHUH
HOOOHUHH~
THEY CAN HOLD UP TO TEN TIMES THEIR BODY WEIGHT IN EMOTIONALLY DEVASTATED PEOPLE.
SMART. SKILLED. LOVING. SO WHY ARE POODLE FANS 68% MORE DEFENSIVE THAN SUPPORTERS OF OTHER BREEDS?
ONE REASON.

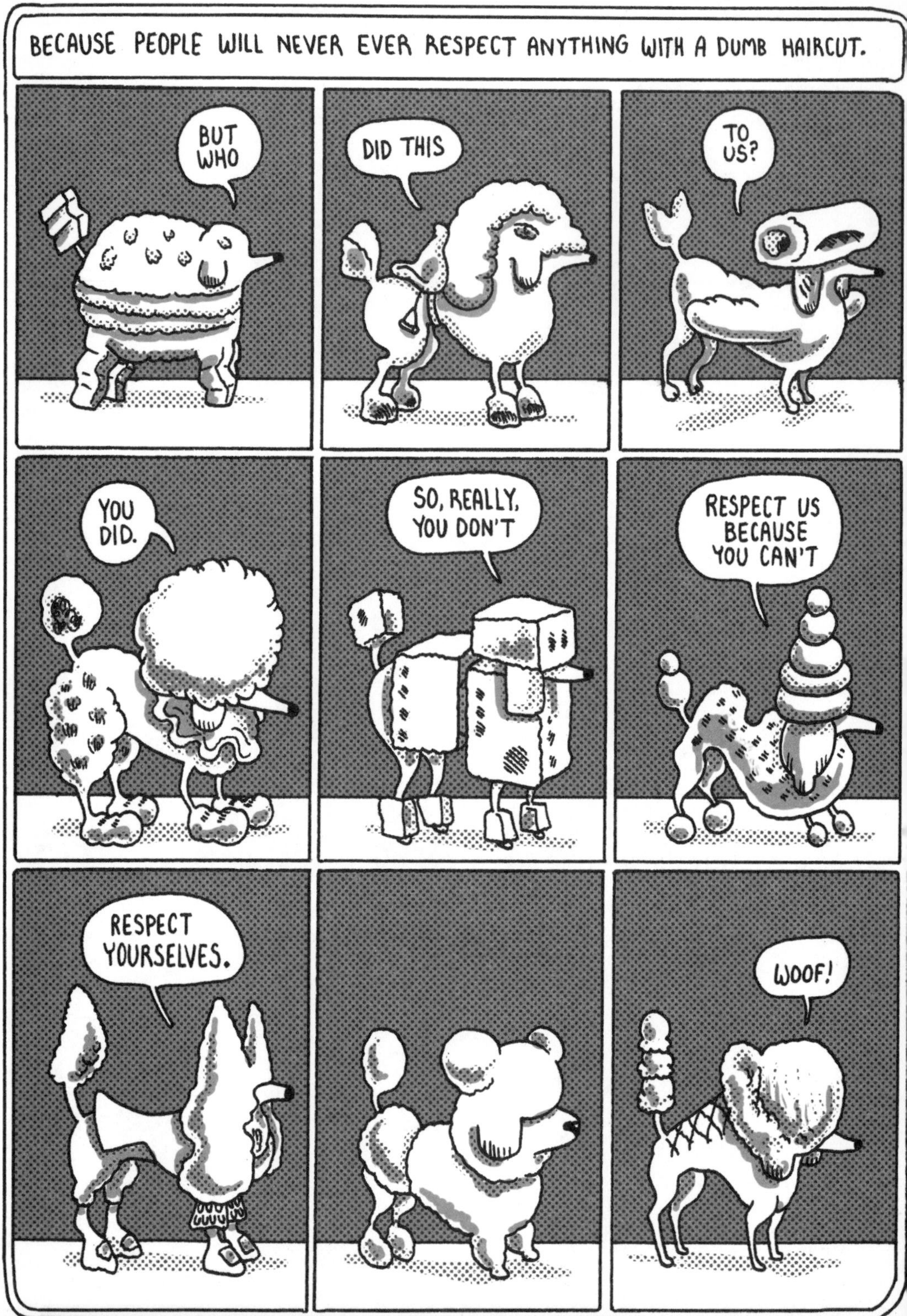
BECAUSE PEOPLE WILL NEVER EVER RESPECT ANYTHING WITH A DUMB HAIRCUT.
BUT WHO
DID THIS
TO US?
YOU DID.
SO, REALLY, YOU DON'T
RESPECT US BECAUSE YOU CAN'T
RESPECT YOURSELVES.
WOOF!

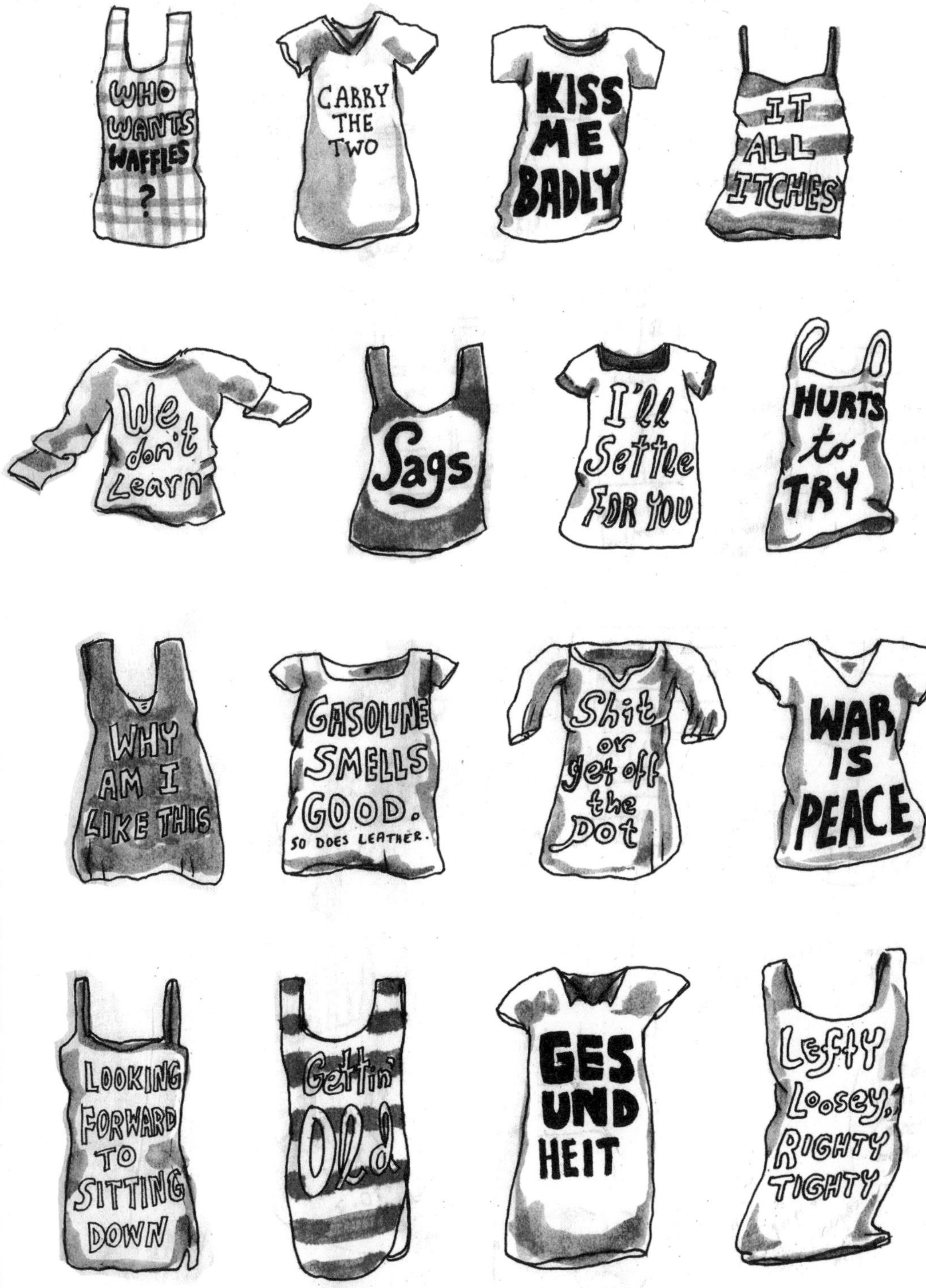
WHO WANTS WAFFLES ?
CARRY THE TWO
KISS ME BADLY
IT ALL ITCHES
We don't Learn
Sags
I'll Settle FOR YOU
HURTS to TRY
WHY AM I LIKE THIS
GASOLINE SMELLS GOOD. SO DOES LEATHER.
Shit or get off the Pot
WAR IS PEACE
LOOKING FORWARD TO SITTING DOWN
Gettin' Old
GES UND HEIT
Lefty Loosey, RIGHTY TIGHTY

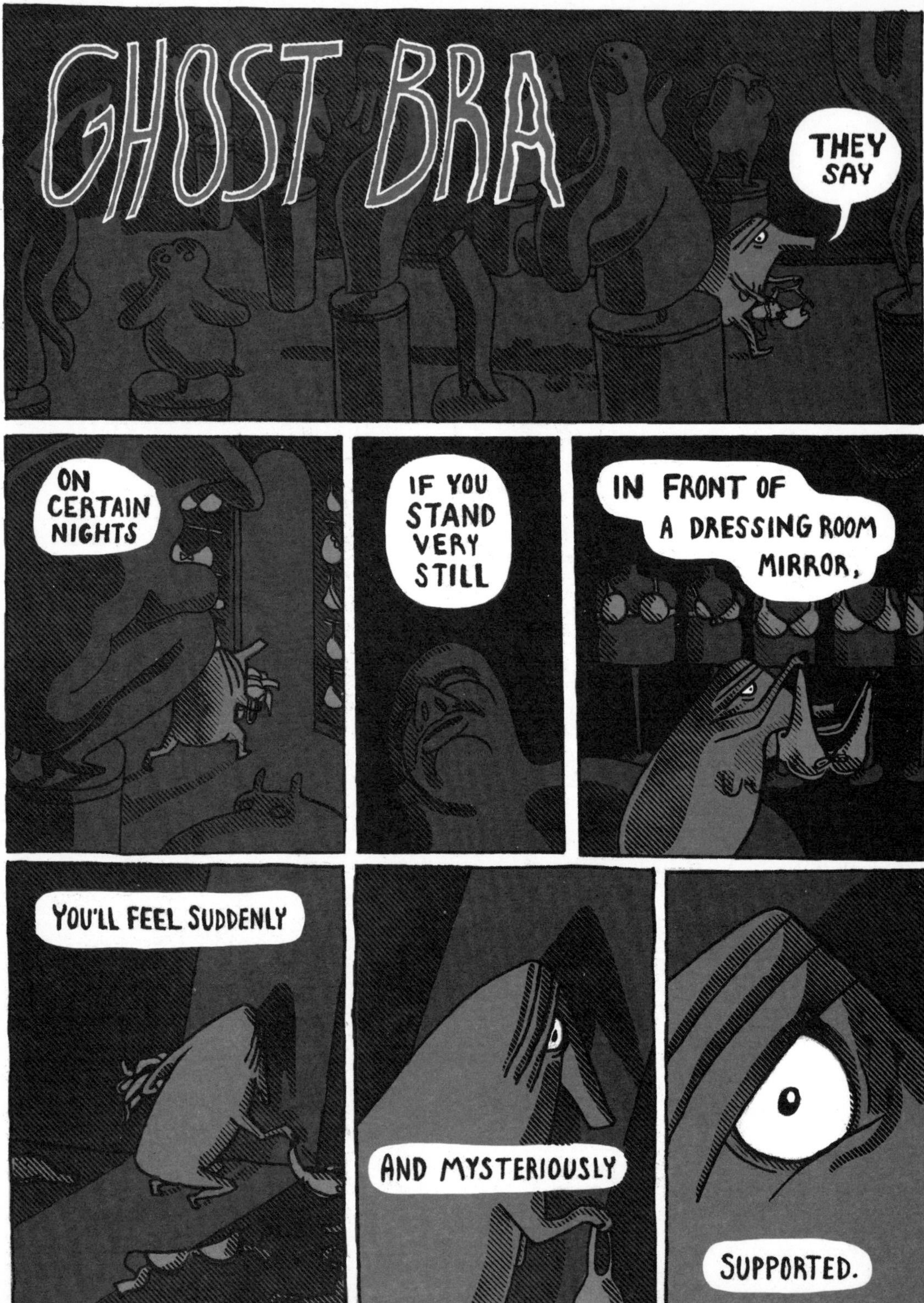
GHOST BRA
THEY SAY
ON CERTAIN NIGHTS
IF YOU STAND VERY STILL
IN FRONT OF A DRESSING ROOM MIRROR,
YOU'LL FEEL SUDDENLY
AND MYSTERIOUSLY
SUPPORTED.

HOW TO POOL:

OUT:

IN:

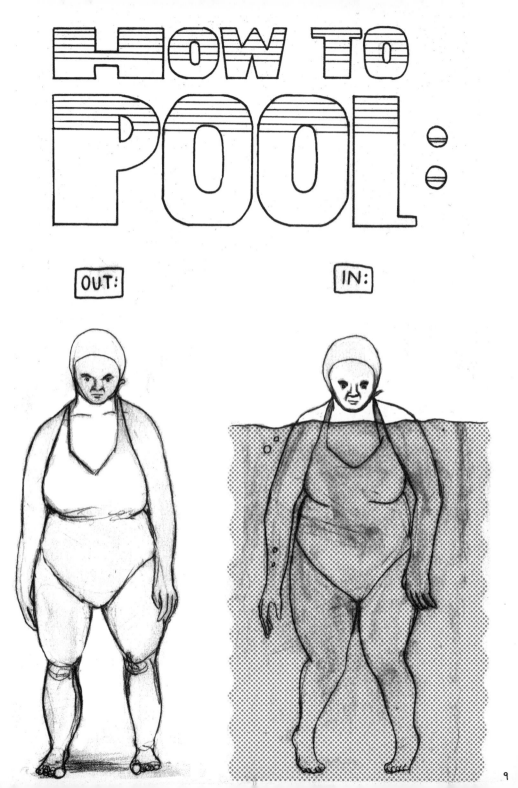

9

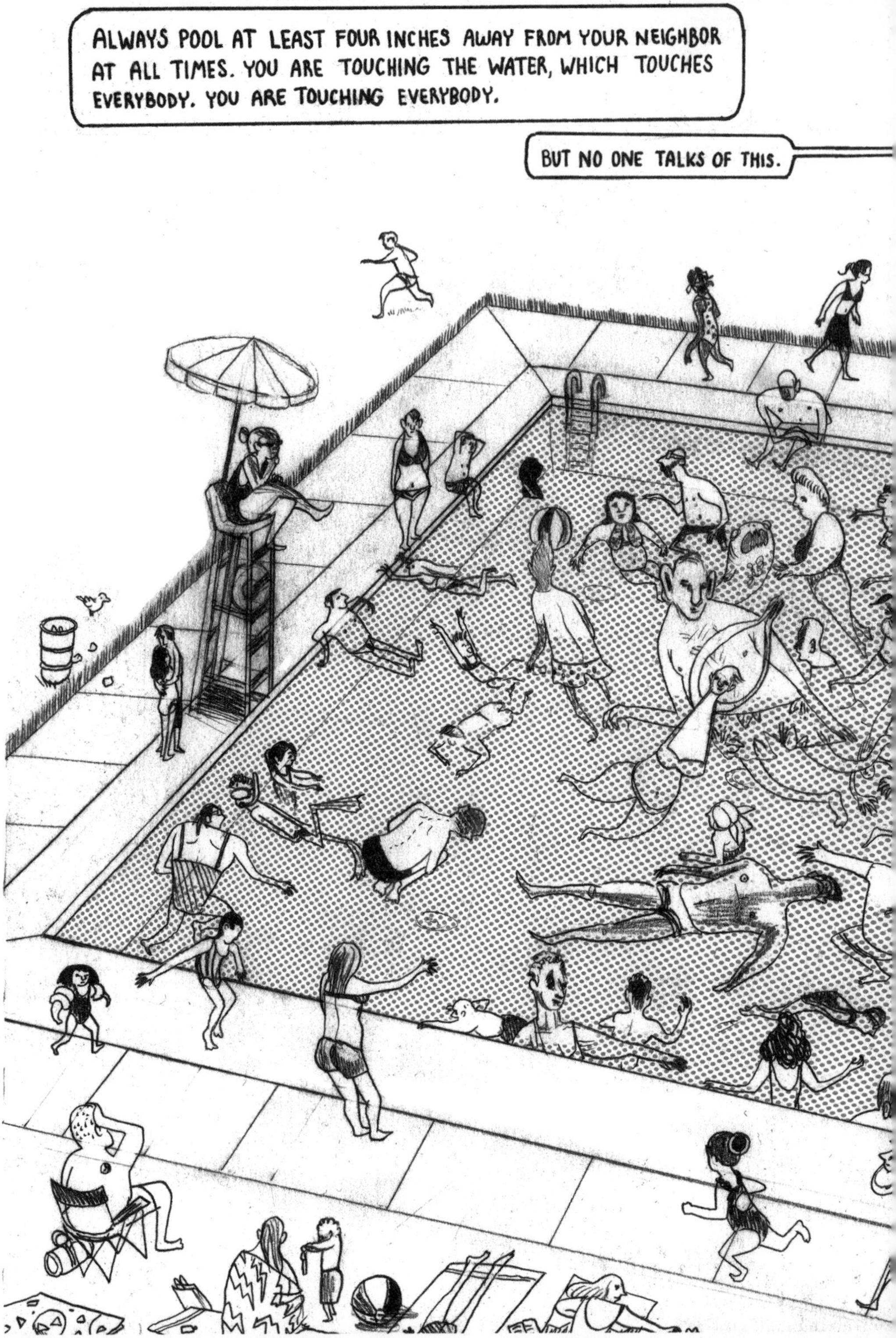
ALWAYS POOL AT LEAST FOUR INCHES AWAY FROM YOUR NEIGHBOR AT ALL TIMES. YOU ARE TOUCHING THE WATER, WHICH TOUCHES EVERYBODY. YOU ARE TOUCHING EVERYBODY.
BUT NO ONE TALKS OF THIS.

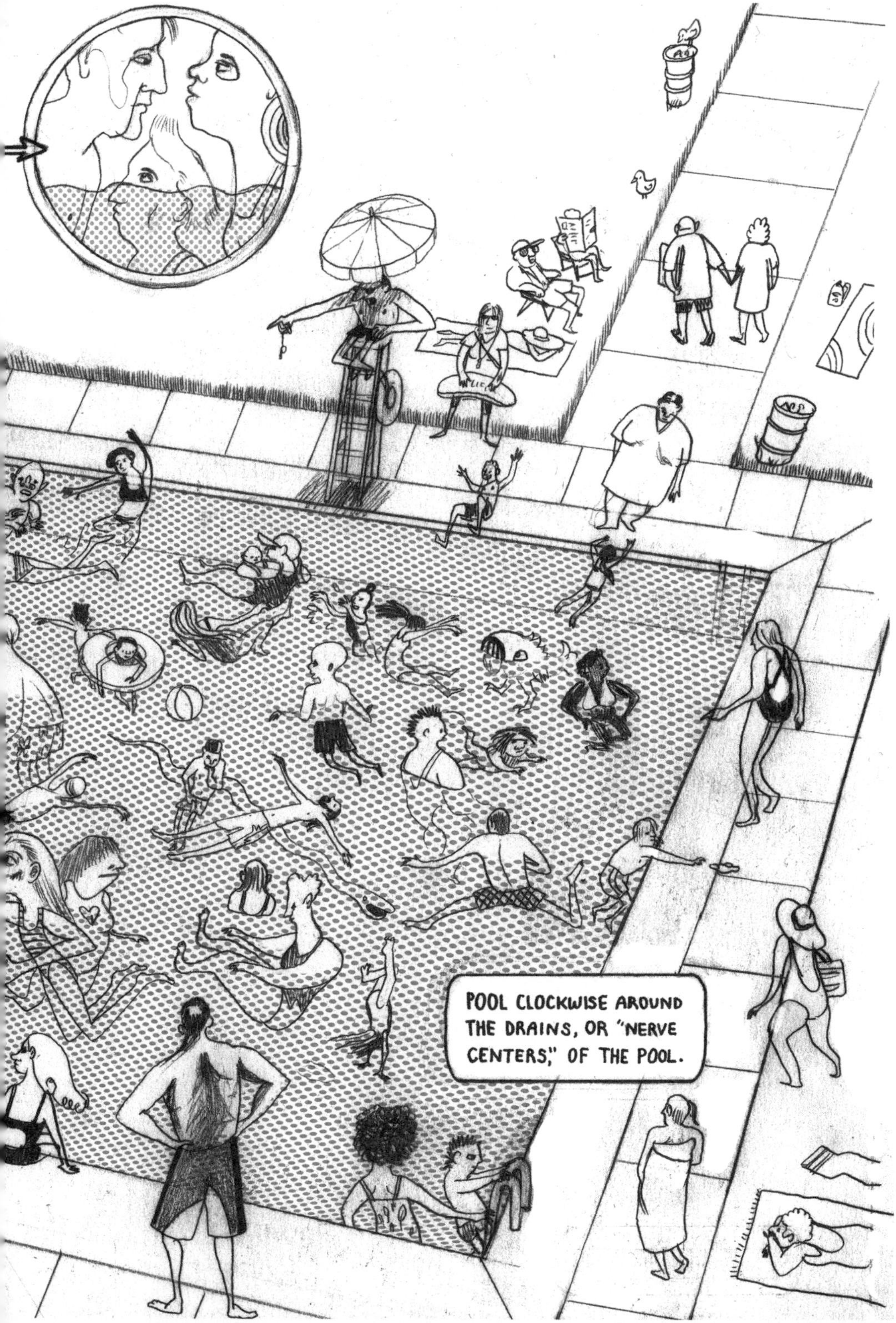
POOL CLOCKWISE AROUND
THE DRAINS, OR "NERVE
CENTERS," OF THE POOL.

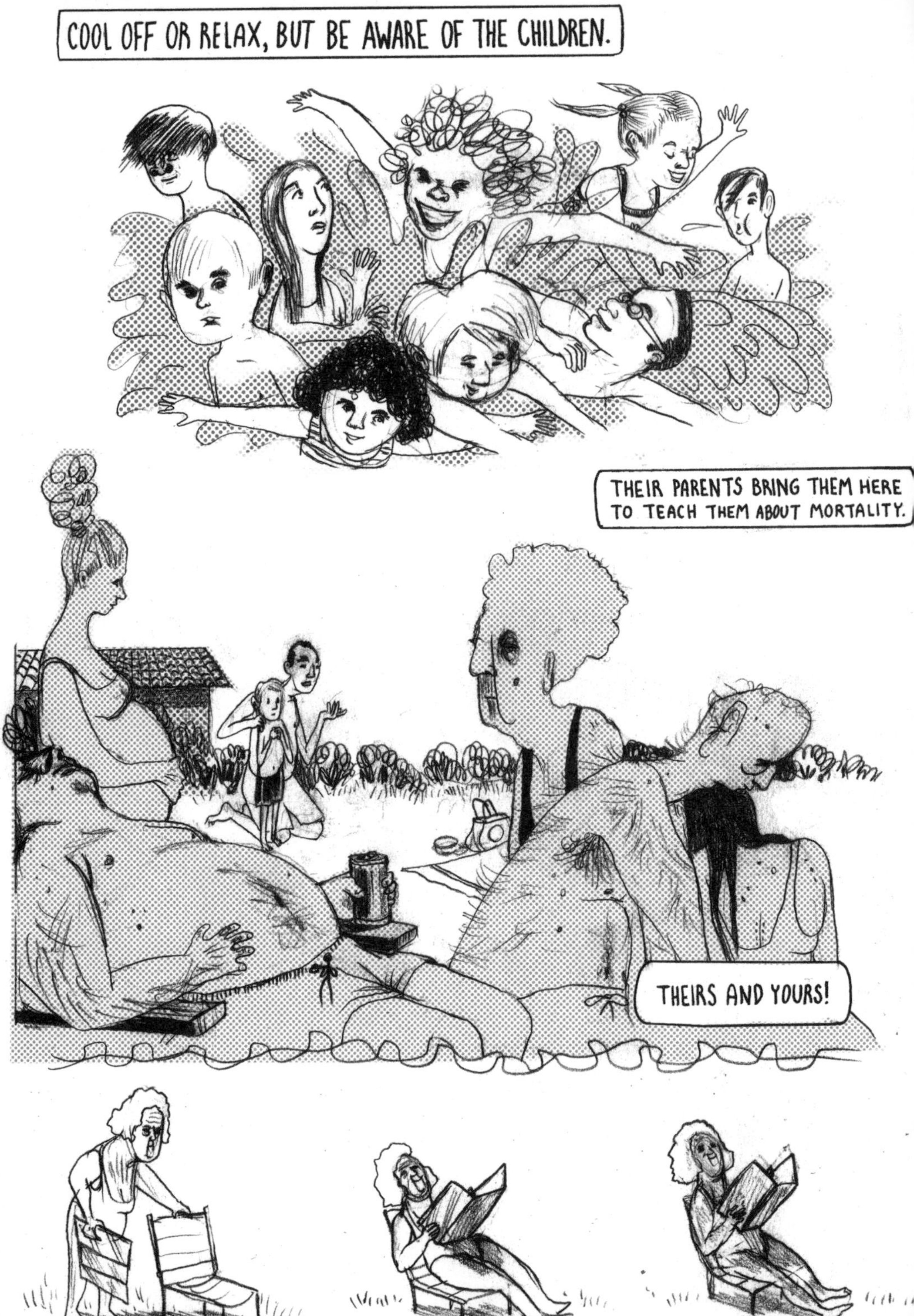
COOL OFF OR RELAX, BUT BE AWARE OF THE CHILDREN.
THEIR PARENTS BRING THEM HERE TO TEACH THEM ABOUT MORTALITY.
THEIRS AND YOURS!

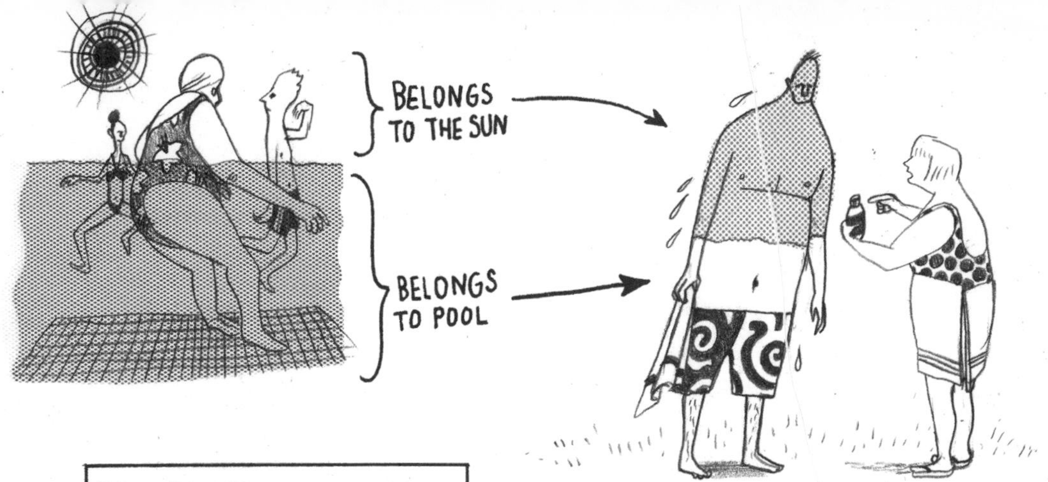
BELONGS TO THE SUN
BELONGS TO POOL

HOW TO POOL OUT OF POOL:

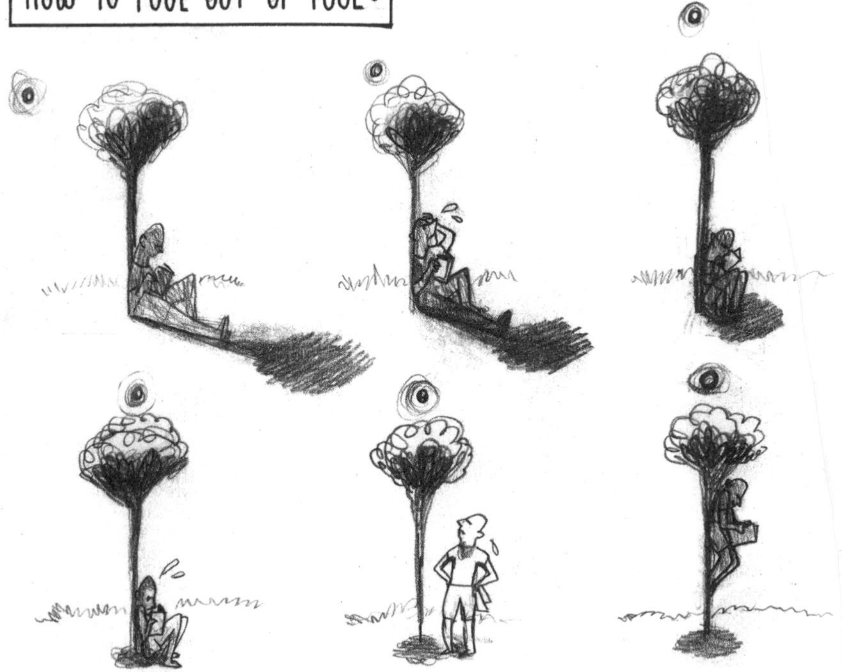

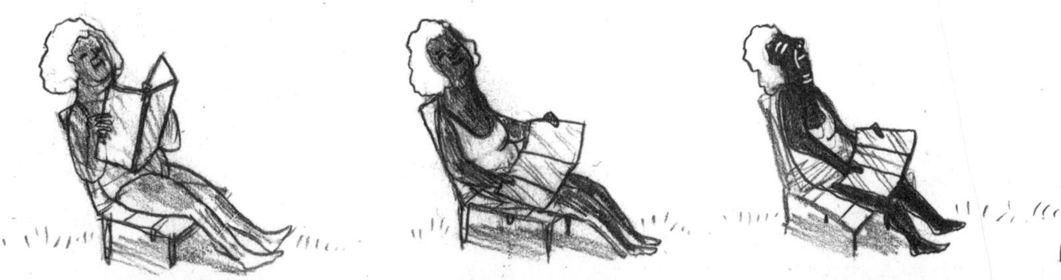

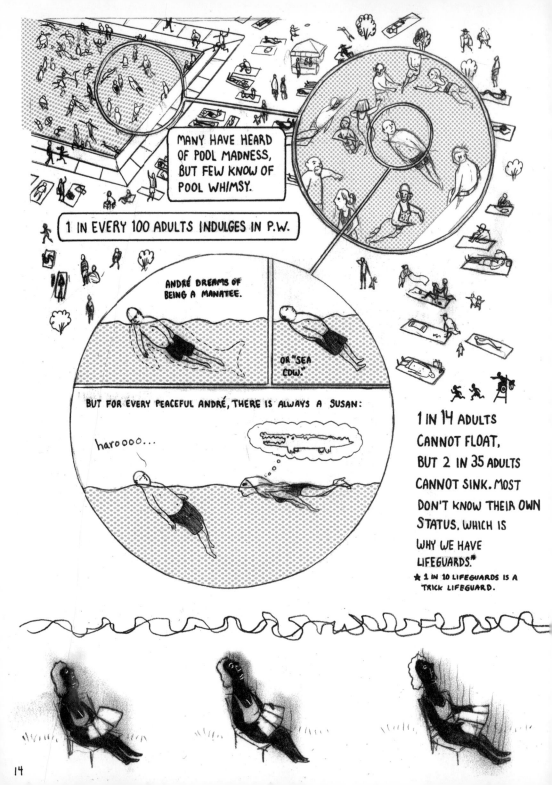

MANY HAVE HEARD OF POOL MADNESS, BUT FEW KNOW OF POOL WHIMSY.

1 IN EVERY 100 ADULTS INDULGES IN P.W.

ANDRÉ DREAMS OF BEING A MANATEE.

OR "SEA COW."

BUT FOR EVERY PEACEFUL ANDRÉ, THERE IS ALWAYS A SUSAN:

haroooo...

1 IN 14 ADULTS CANNOT FLOAT, BUT 2 IN 35 ADULTS CANNOT SINK. MOST DON'T KNOW THEIR OWN STATUS, WHICH IS WHY WE HAVE LIFEGUARDS.*

★ 1 IN 10 LIFEGUARDS IS A TRICK LIFEGUARD.

WATCH HOW YOUR FEELINGS ABOUT POOLING CHANGE AS YOU GROW UP.

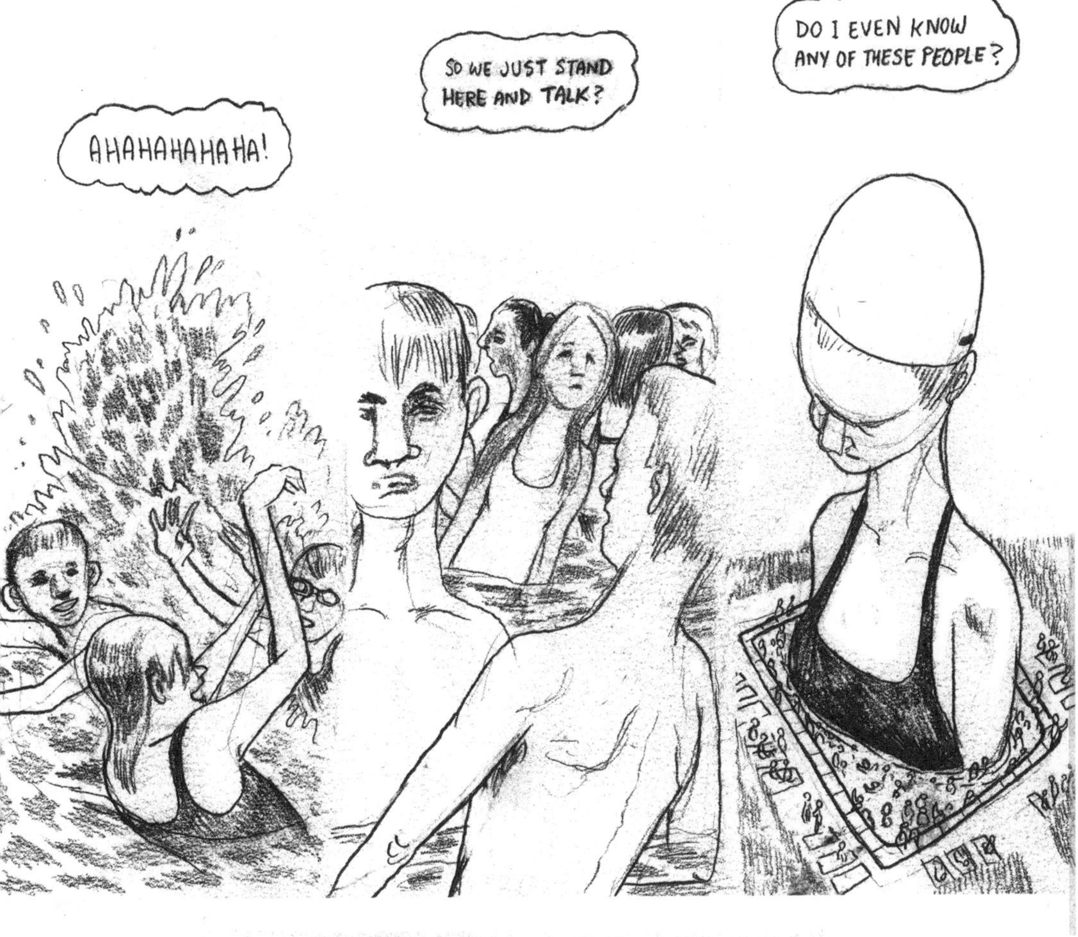
AHAHAHAHAHA!
SO WE JUST STAND HERE AND TALK?
DO I EVEN KNOW ANY OF THESE PEOPLE?

WHEN DONE RIGHT, POOLING IS ITS OWN REWARD!

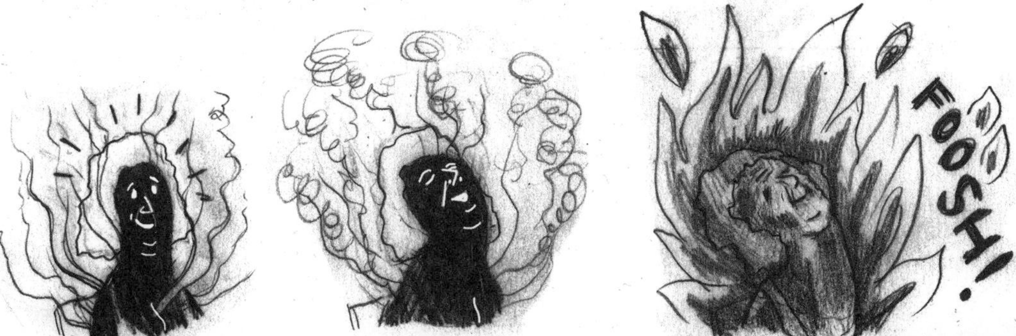
FOOSH!

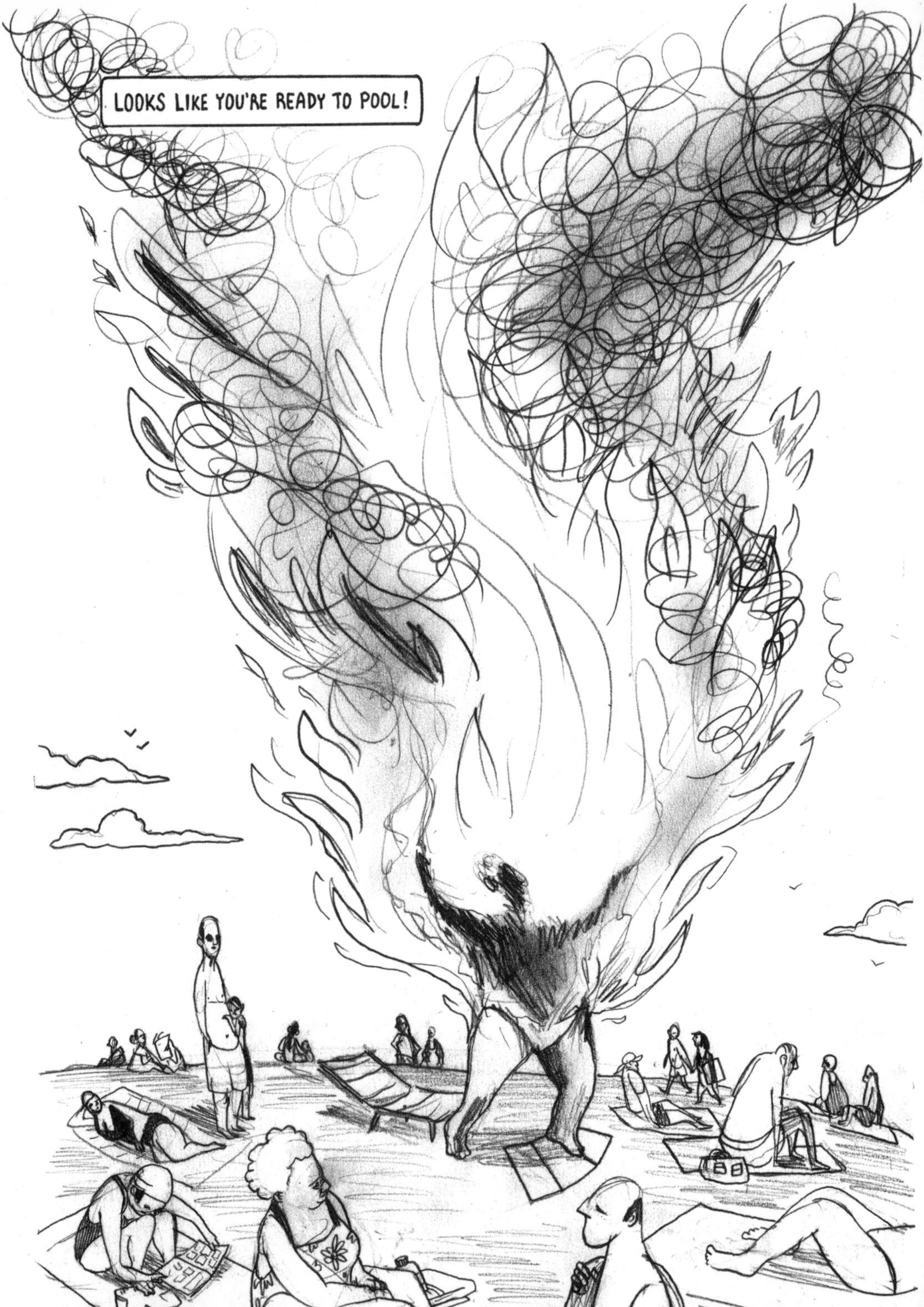
LOOKS LIKE YOU'RE READY TO POOL!

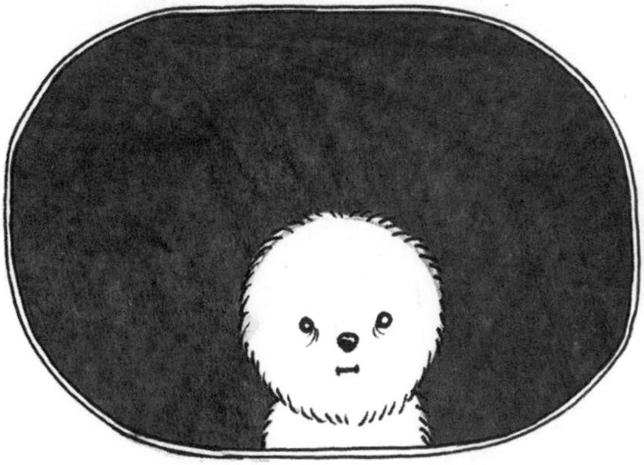

•BICHON•

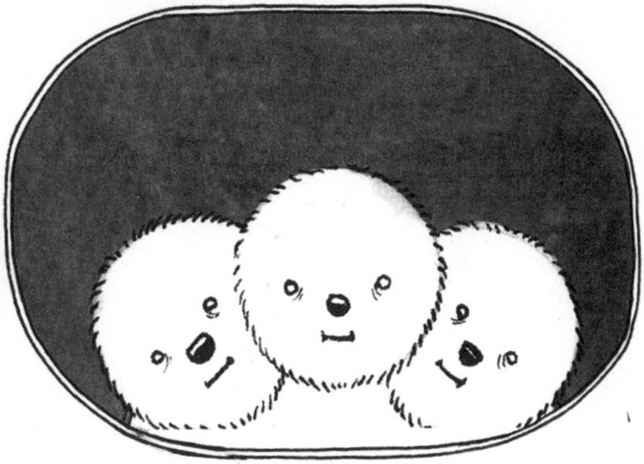

•TRICHON•

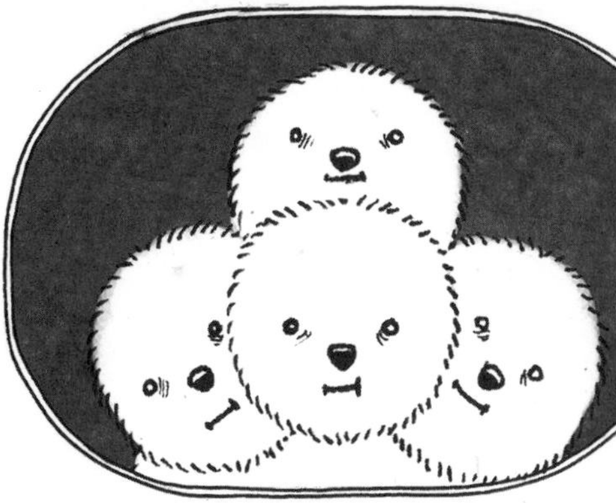

•TETRACHON•

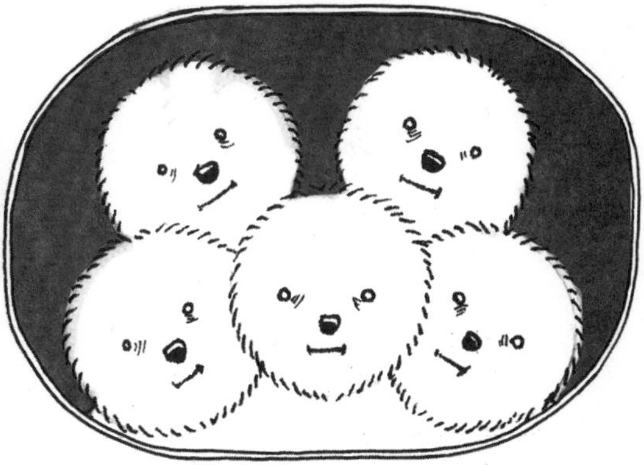

•PENTACHON•

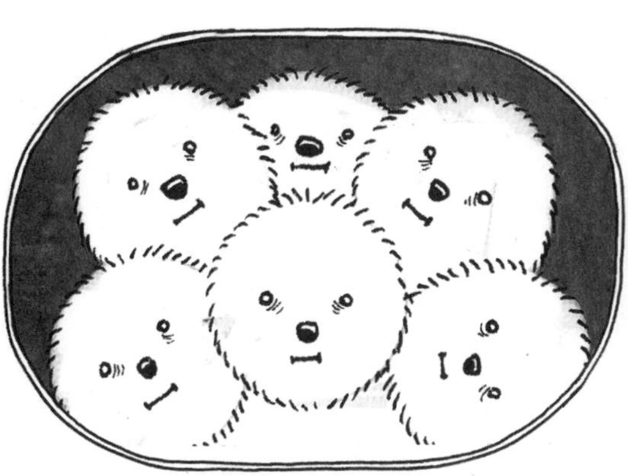

•HEXACHON•

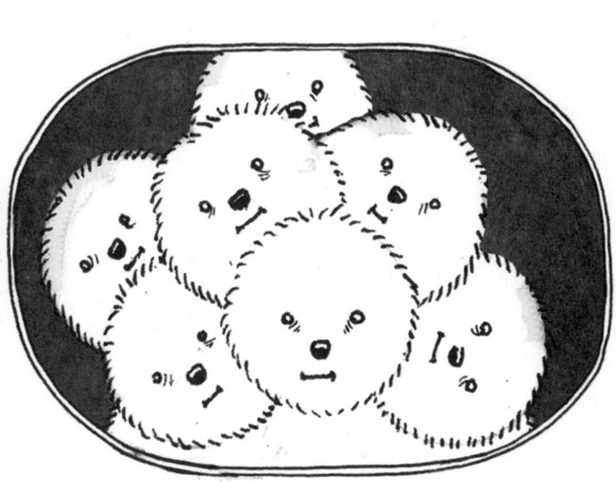

•HEPTACHON•

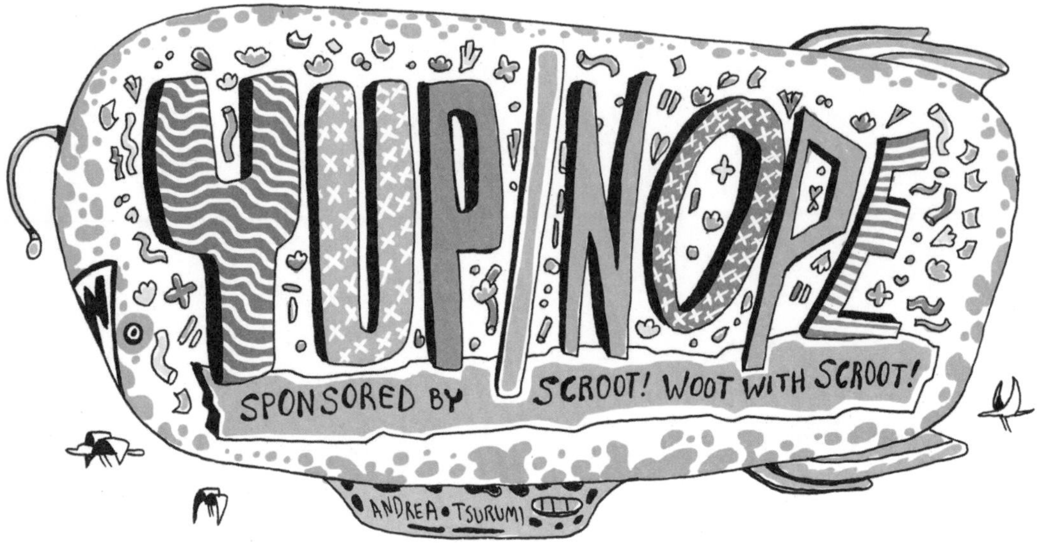
YUP/NOPE
SPONSORED BY SCROOT! WOOT WITH SCROOT!
ANDREA • TSURUMI

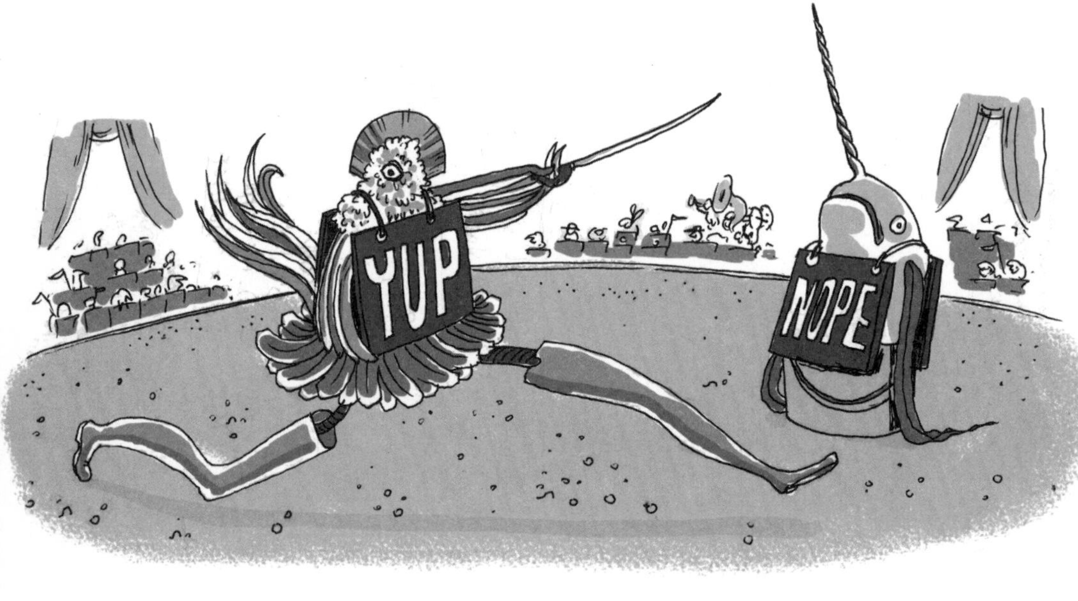
YUP
NOPE

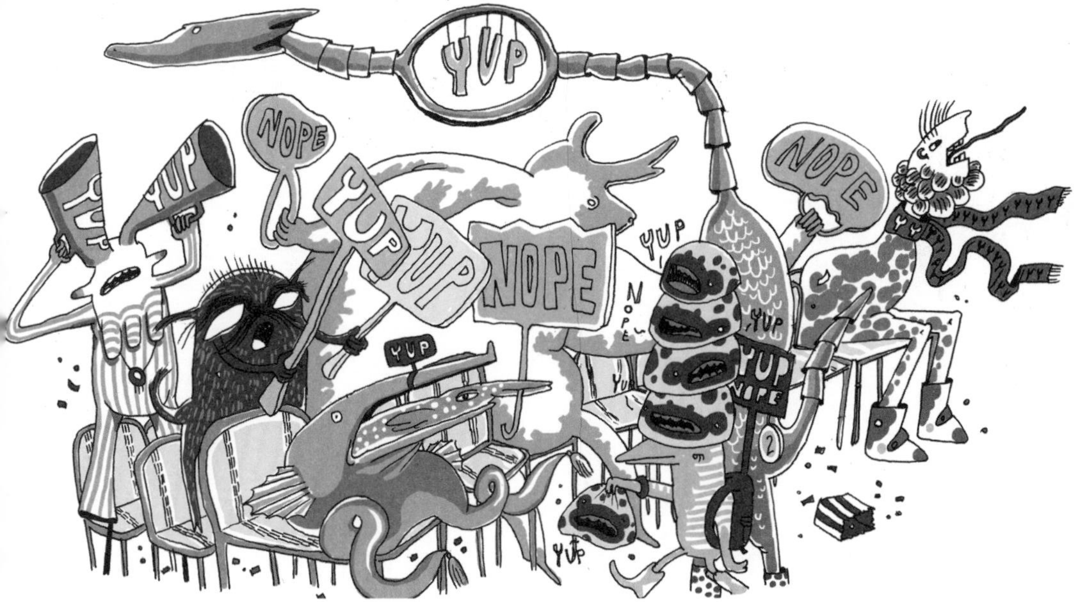
YUP
NOPE
YUP
YUP
YUP
YUP
NOPE
YUP
NOPE
YUP
YUP
NOPE
YUP
YUP

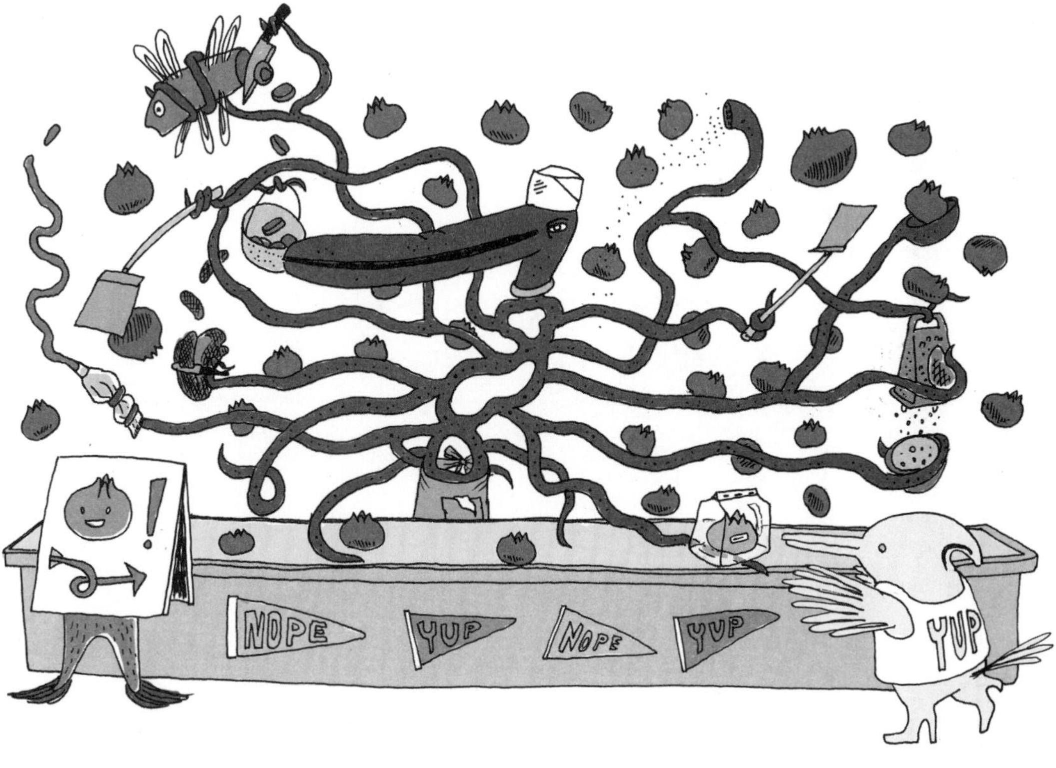
!
NOPE
YUP
NOPE
YUP
YUP

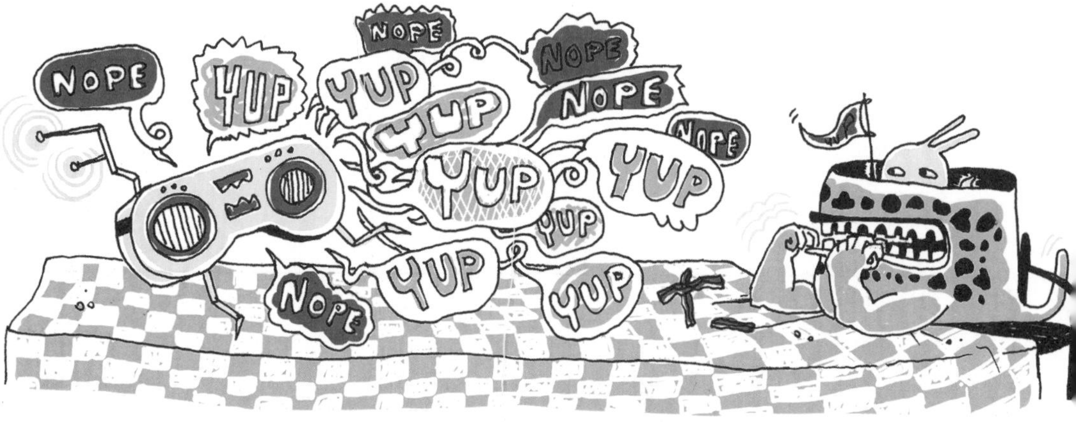
NOPE
YUP
NOPE
YUP
YUP
NOPE
NOPE
NOPE
YUP
YUP
YUP
NOPE
YUP
YUP

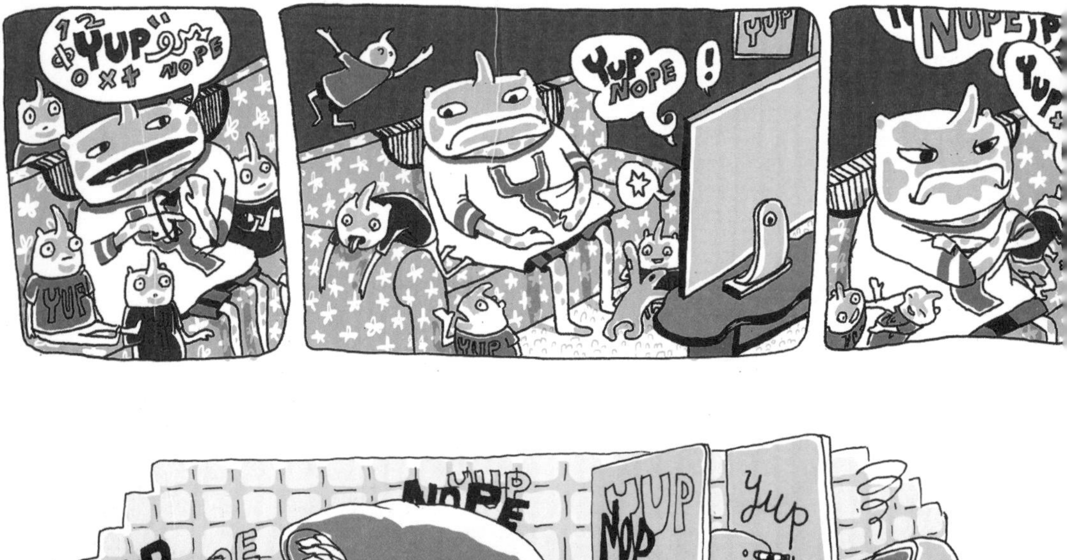
YUP NOPE
YUP
YUP NOPE !
YUP
NOPE
YUP

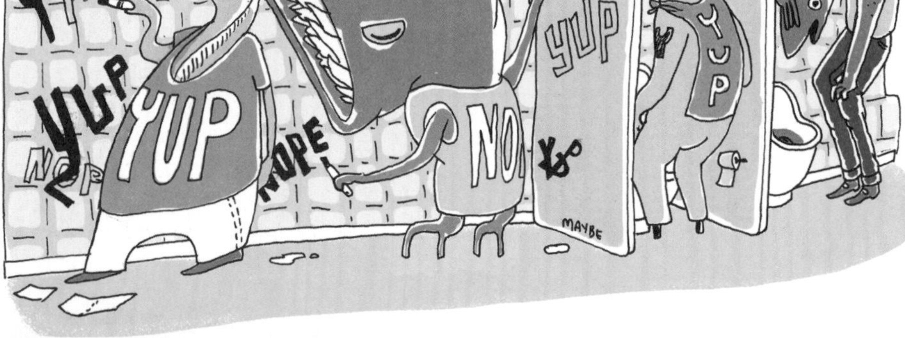
NOPE
YUP
YUP
NOPE
YUP
YUP
YUP
NOPE
YUP
yup
YUP
YUP
NO
MAYBE

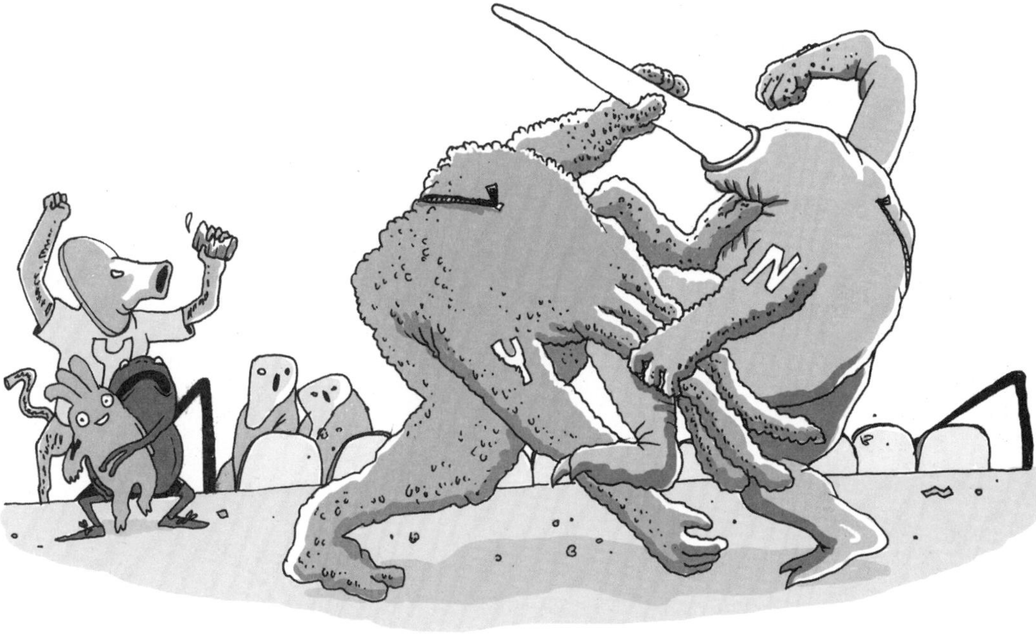

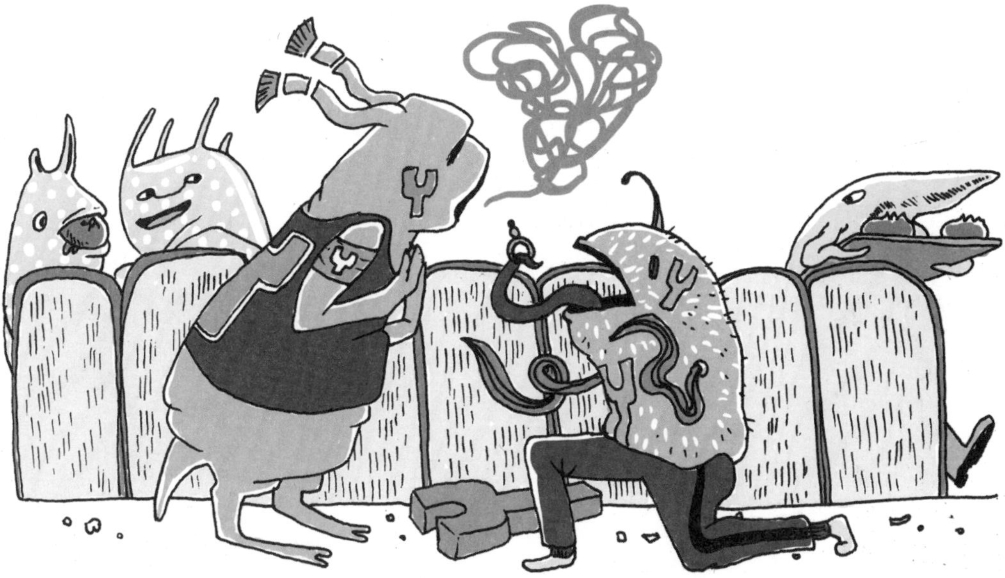

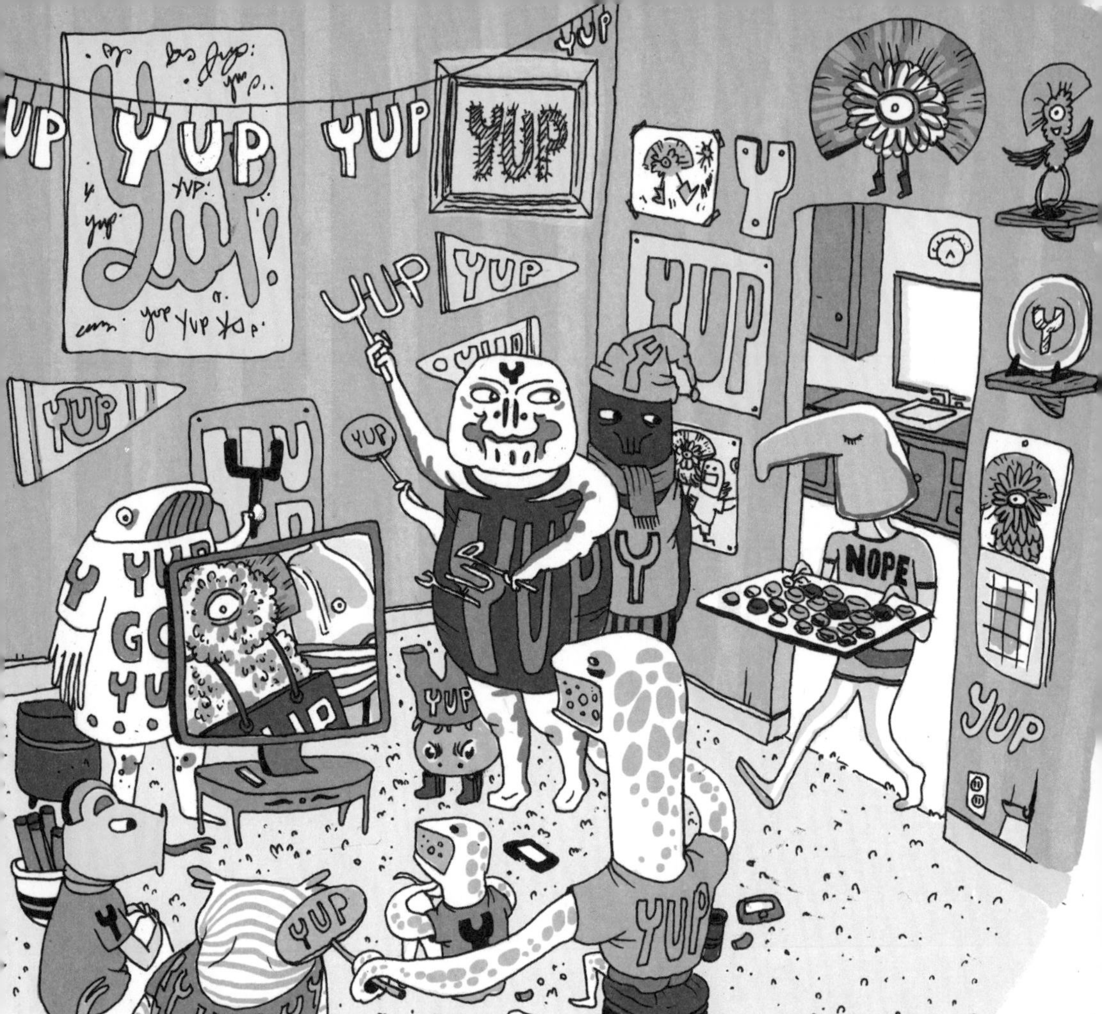

YUP
YUP
YUP
YUP
YUP
YUP
YUP
YUP
YUP GO YU
NOPE
YUP
YUP
YUP
YUP

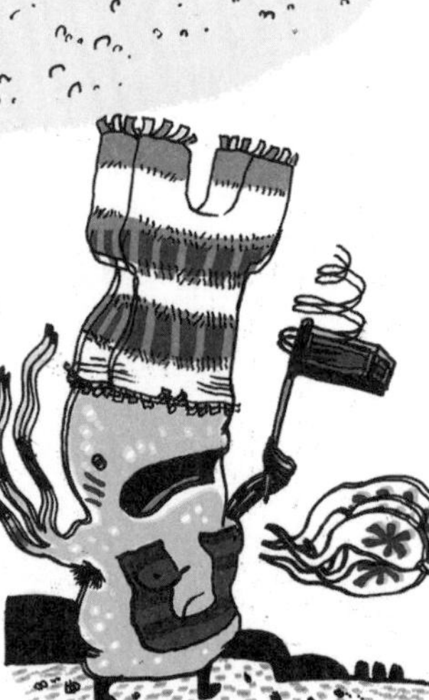

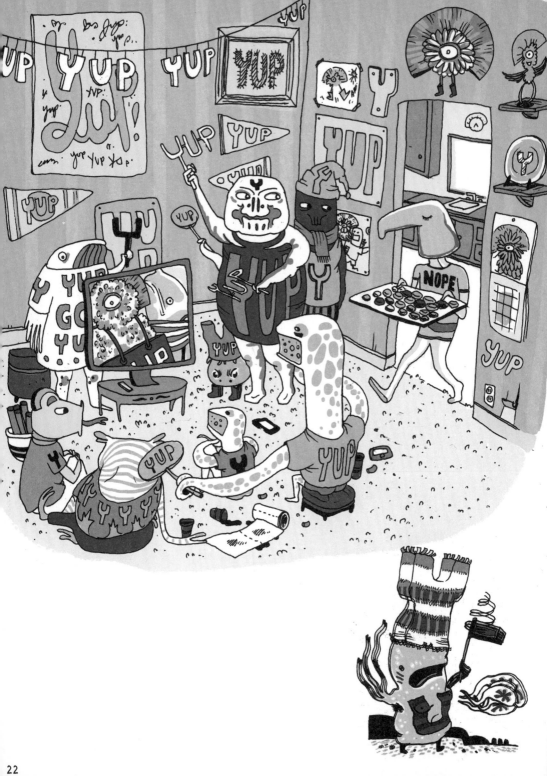

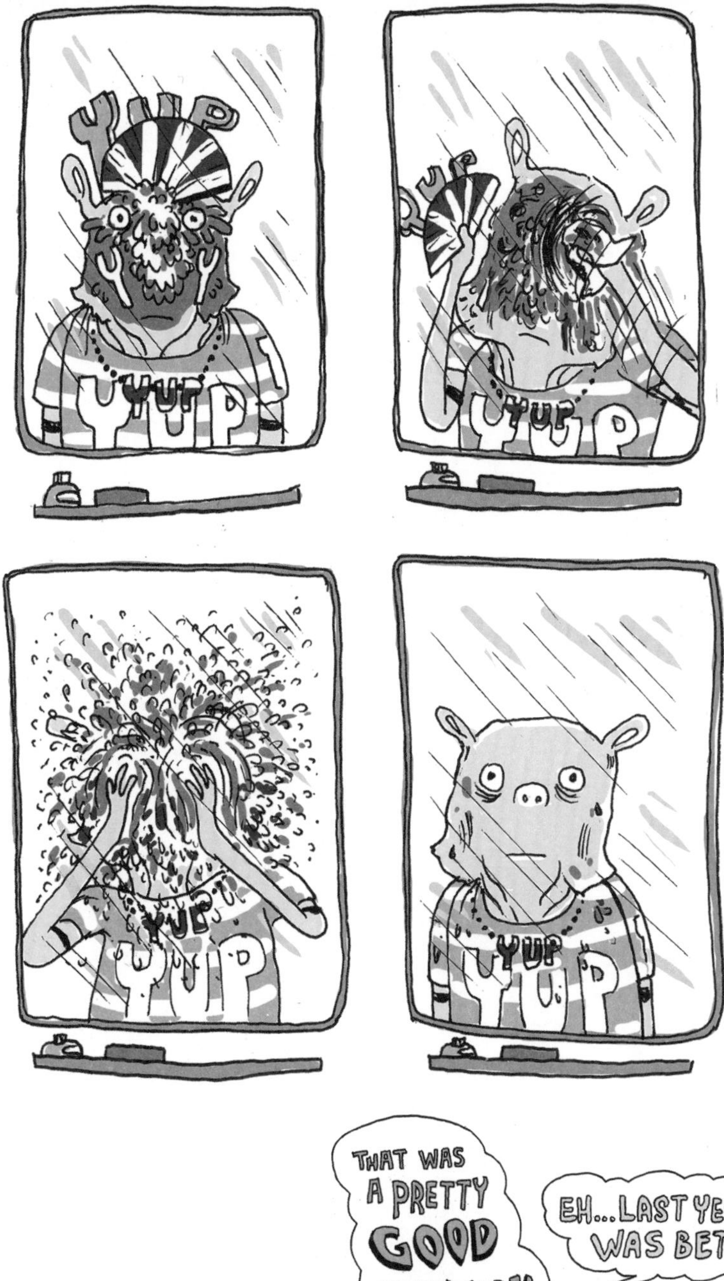
THAT WAS A PRETTY GOOD YUP/NOPE!
EH... LAST YEAR'S WAS BETTER.

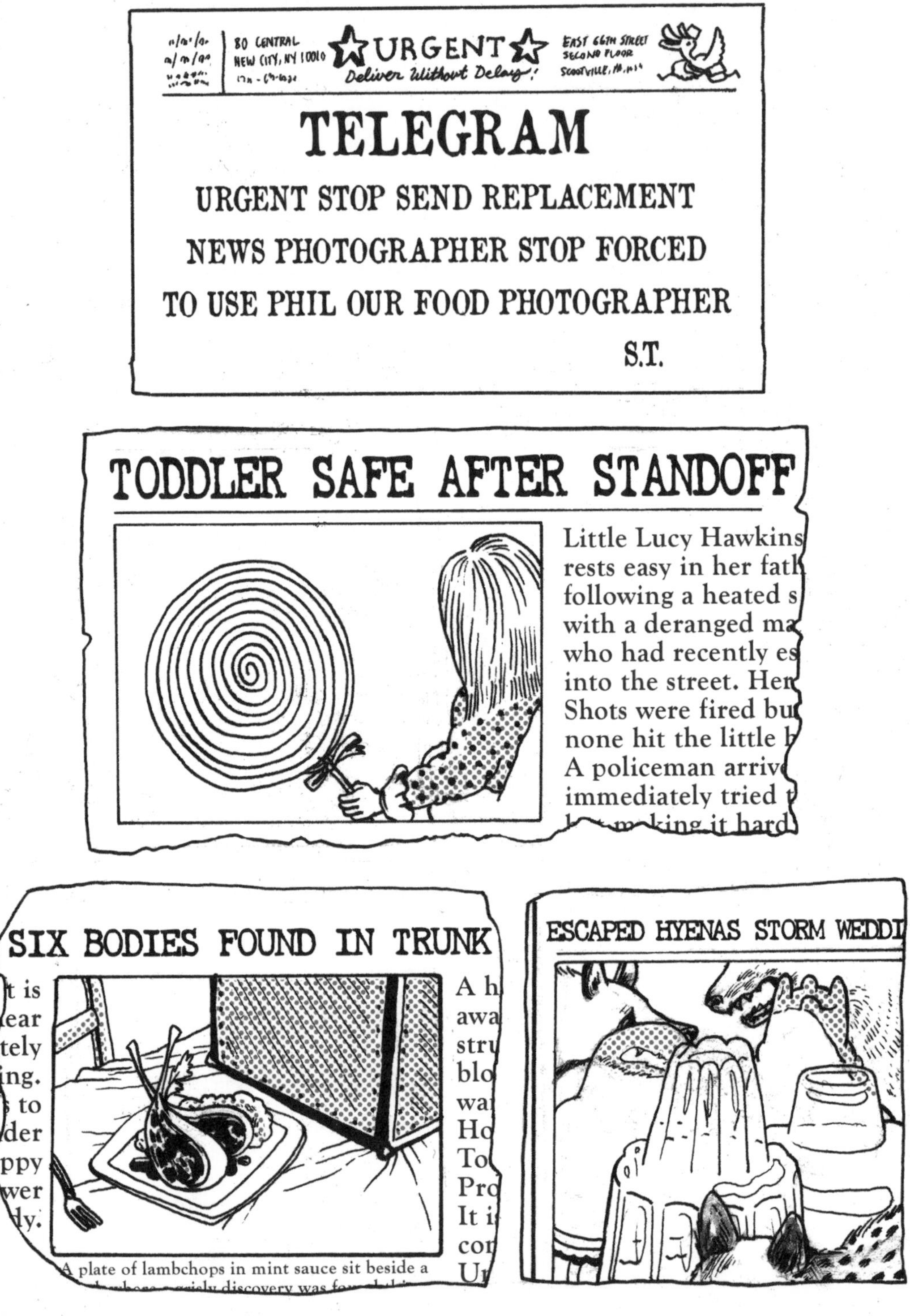
80 CENTRAL
NEW CITY, NY 10010
URGENT
Deliver Without Delay!
EAST 66TH STREET
SECOND FLOOR
TELEGRAM
URGENT STOP SEND REPLACEMENT
NEWS PHOTOGRAPHER STOP FORCED
TO USE PHIL OUR FOOD PHOTOGRAPHER
S.T.
TODDLER SAFE AFTER STANDOFF
Little Lucy Hawkins
rests easy in her
following a heated
with a deranged
who had recently
into the street.
Shots were fired
none hit the little
A policeman
immediately tried
SIX BODIES FOUND IN TRUNK
is
ear
tely
ing.
to
der
ppy
wer
dy.
A plate of lambchops in mint sauce sit beside a
ESCAPED HYENAS STORM

U.S.S.R. JOINS ALLIED FORCES IN NEW CAMPAIGN

Churchill and Stalin shake hands by this superb rigatoni with tomatoes, capers, and olives. Hopes rise that this momentous decision will turn the tide in an increasingly desperate campaign across the continent. Reporters tried to ascertain if

CAUGHT RED-HANDED! SEX PART[

A v
at
gu
Ra
on
Po
Ho
to
for
un
sca
un
Ho

A raspberry-gin fizz tumbles wildly as Nick Scoobie makes

CONEY ISL. MASSACRE CLAIMS EIGHT LIVES

Candy corn, a simple yet wholesome treat, lie scattered across the boardwalk on a sunny summer day marred by tragedy. Witnesses say

FIRE RAGES IN 6TH DISTRICT
Fire Crews Work 12 Hour Shifts; National

Of
th
W
th
try
bu
it
to
N
bo
t
tr
pu
th

A brave apple crumble stands alone in the inferno ragin

SCIENTIFIC BREAKT[

A chicken parm submarine sandwich sits forgotten in the lab as the Montreal team celebrates their miraculous discovery of the N-12 particle, a feat long considered impossible by top scientists around the world. A recent breakthrough proved otherwise in momentous occasion. The prime minister calls

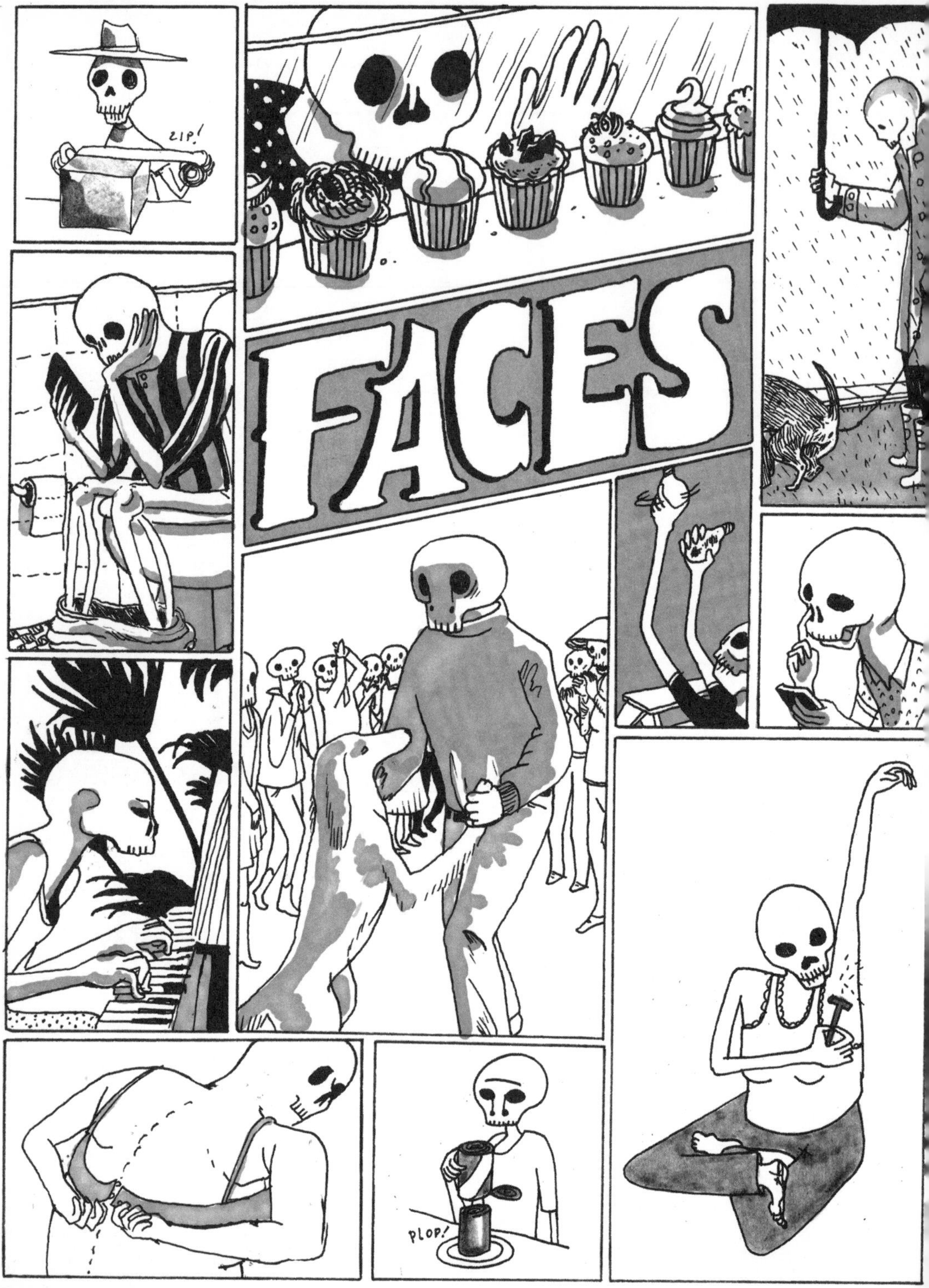
ZIP!
FACES
PLOP!

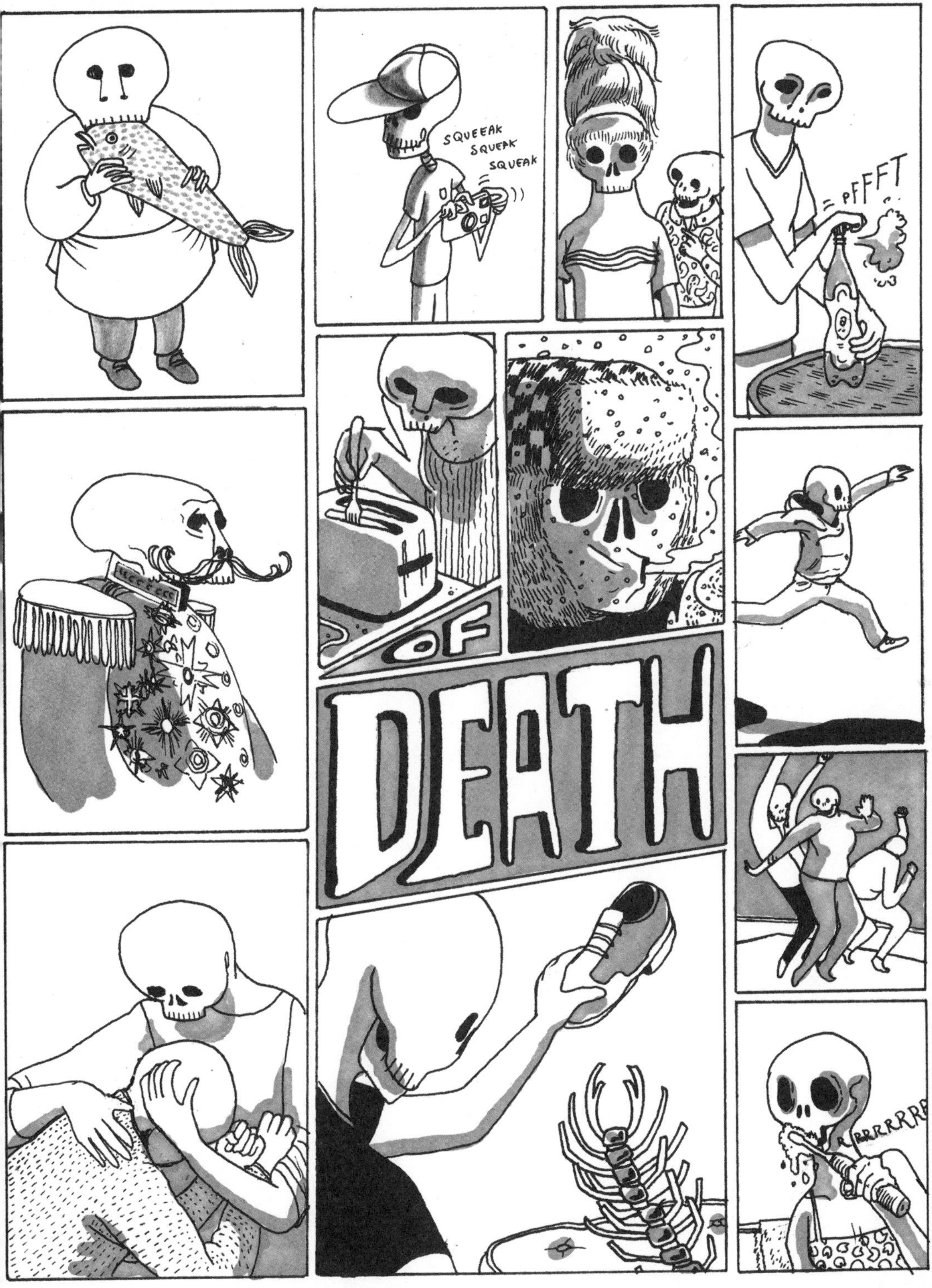
SQUEEAK
SQUEAK
SQUEAK
pFFFT
OF
DEATH
RRRRRRR

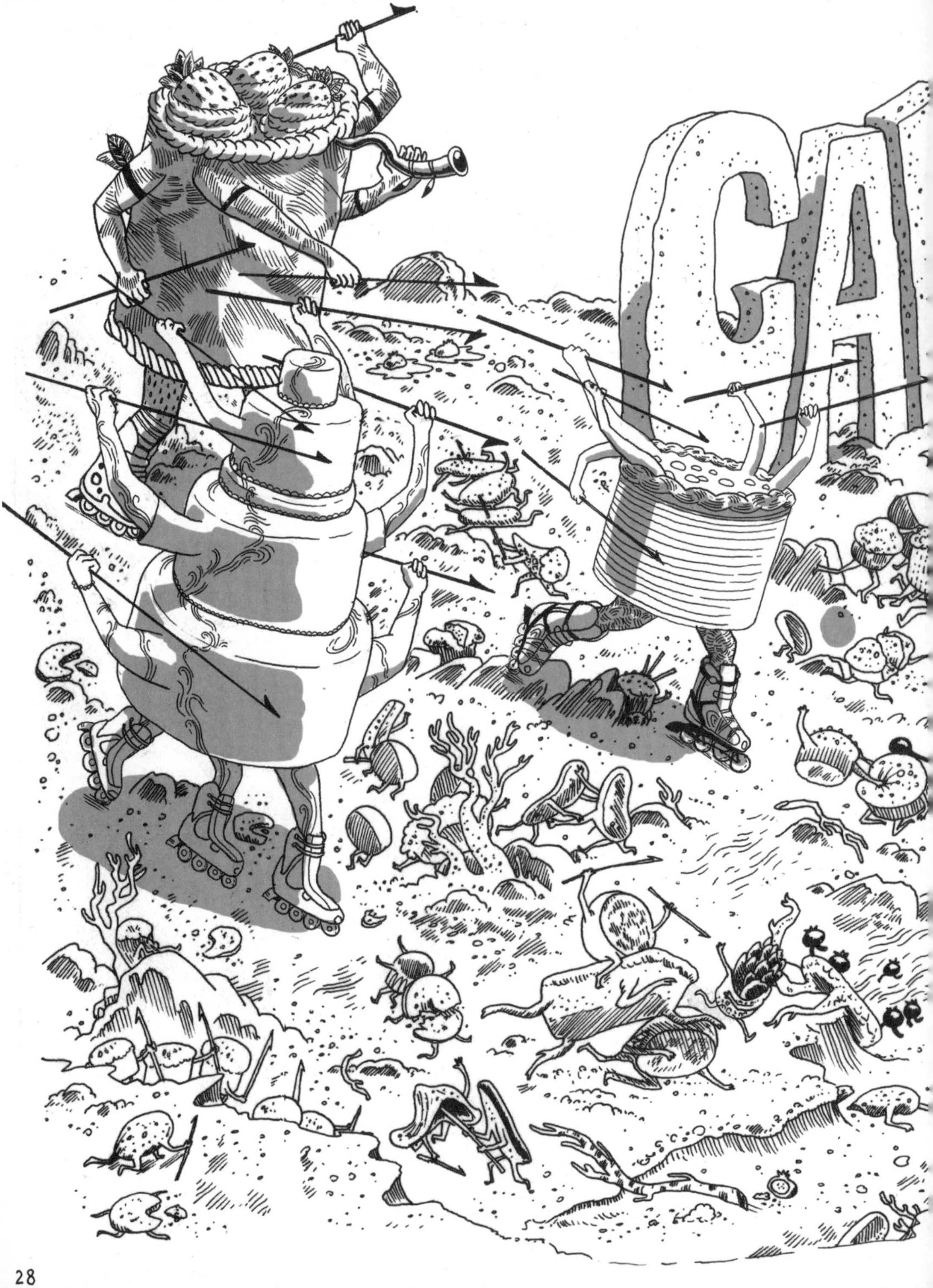
CA

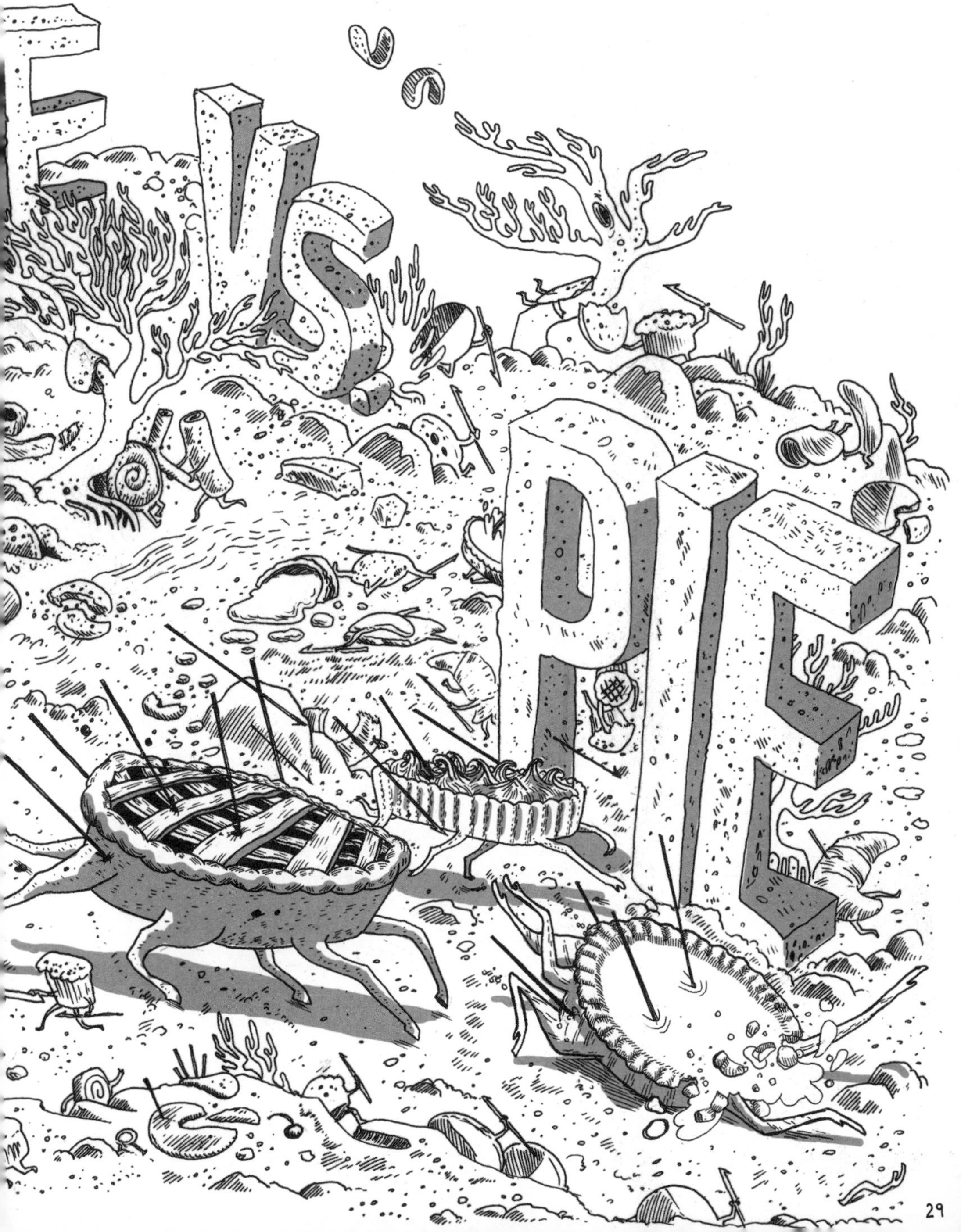
E VS.
PIE

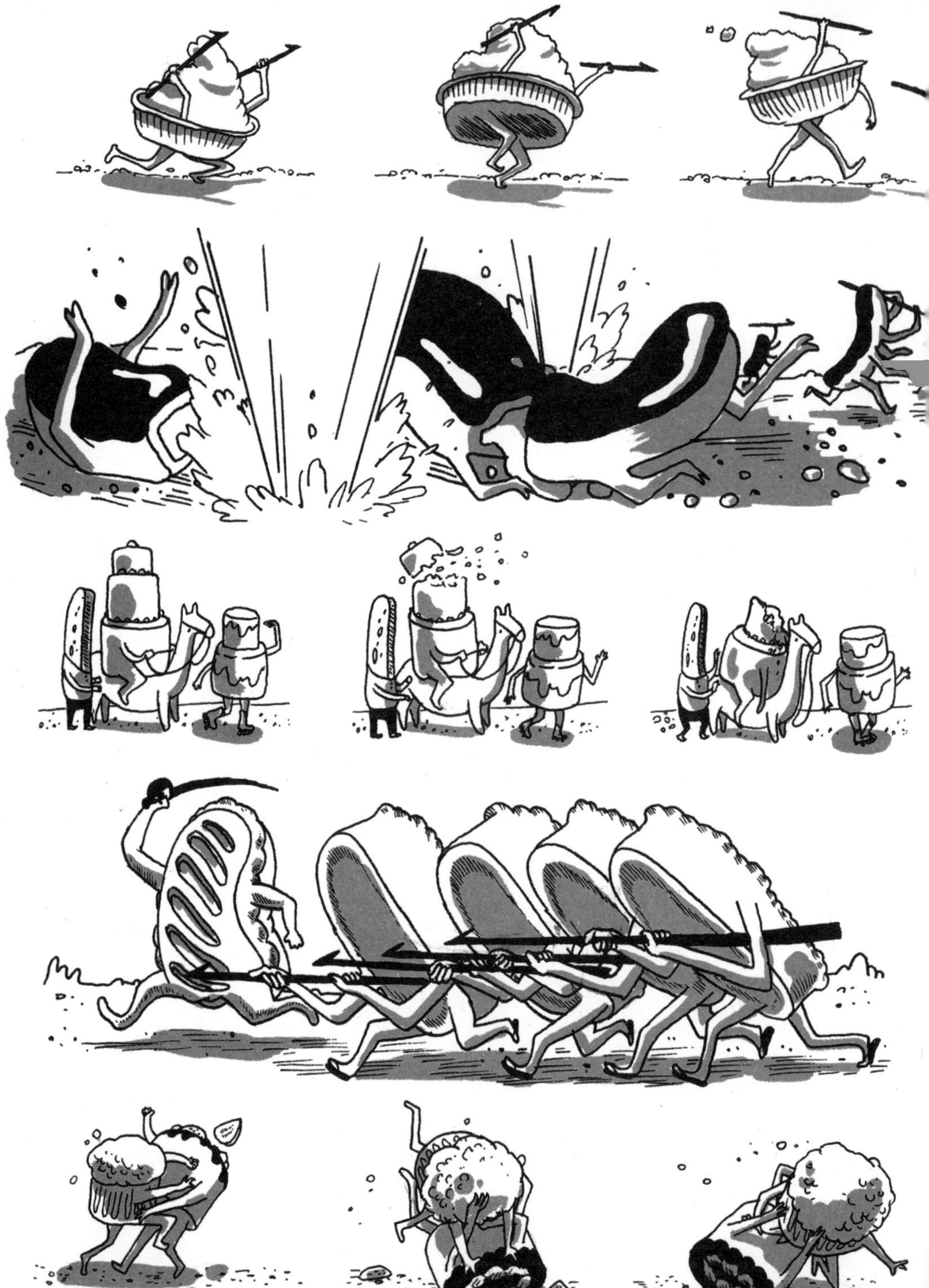

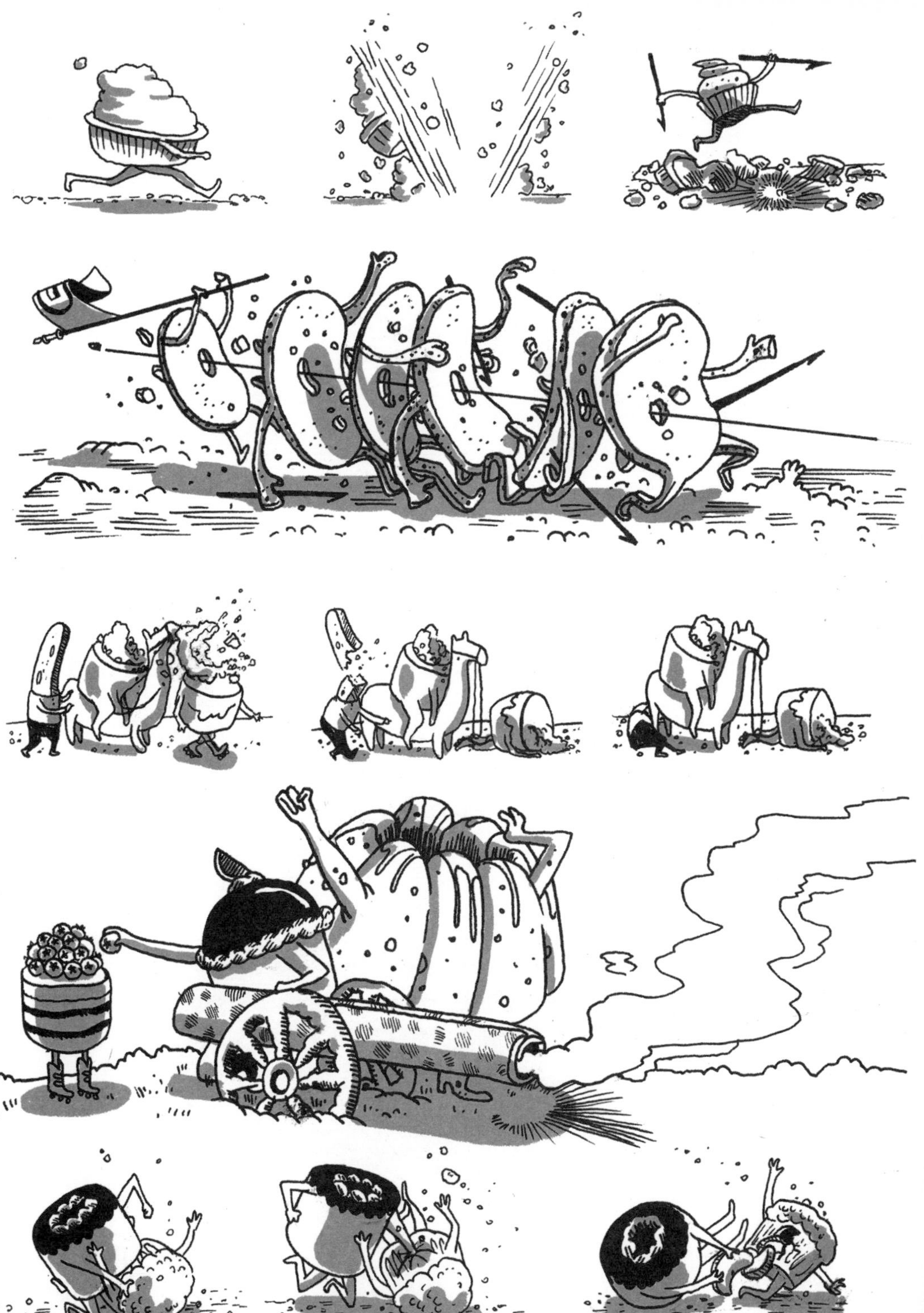

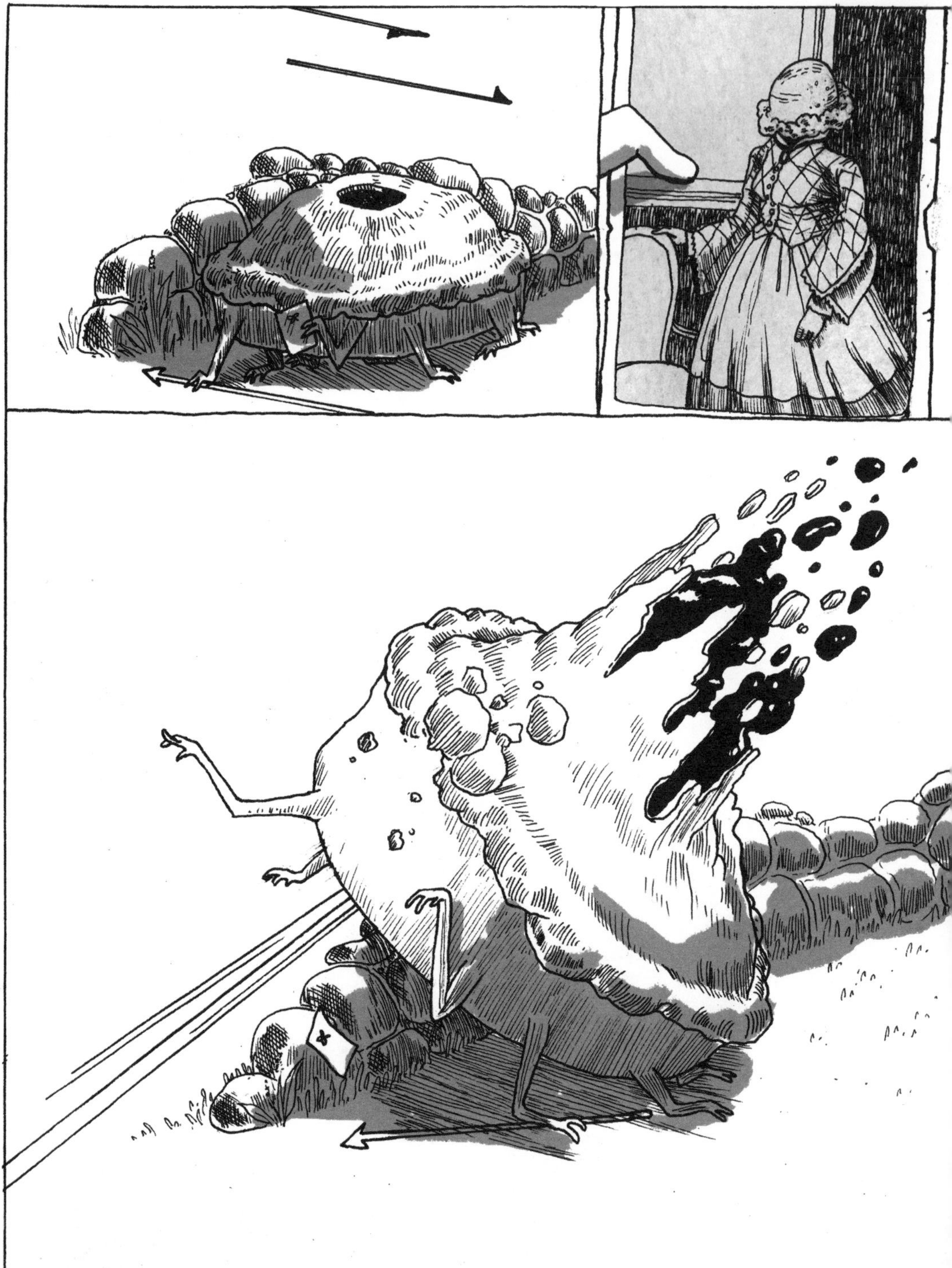

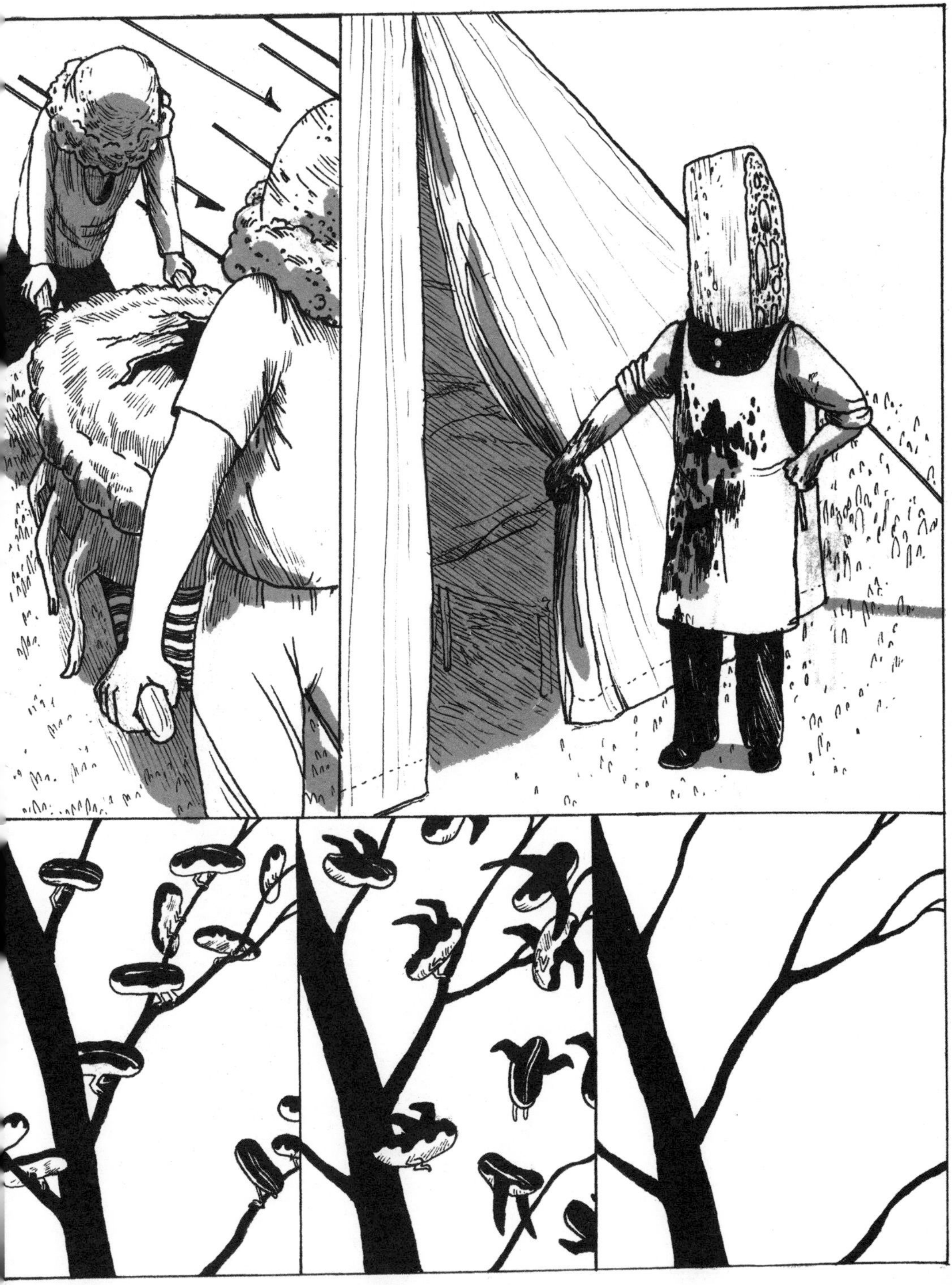

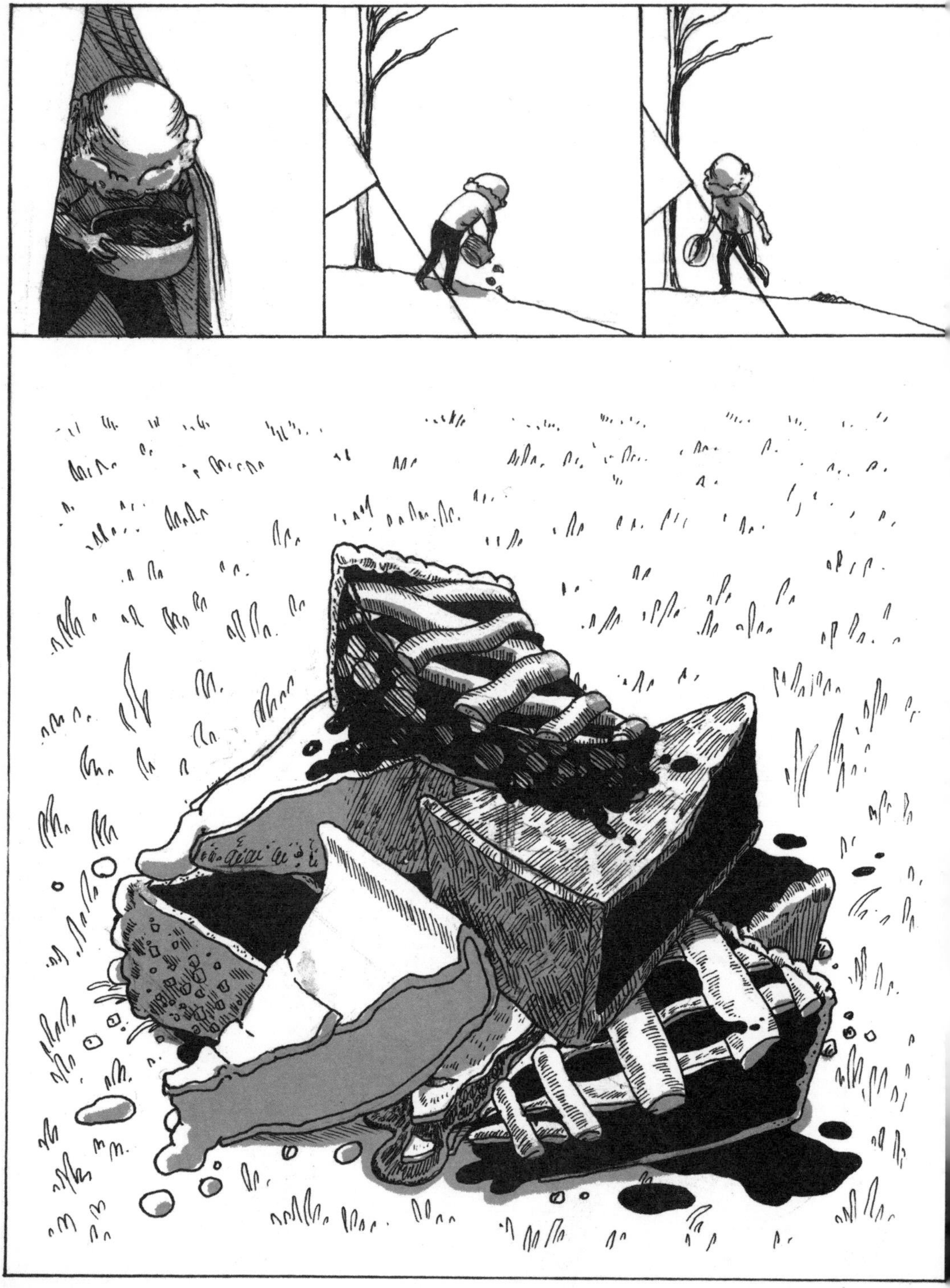

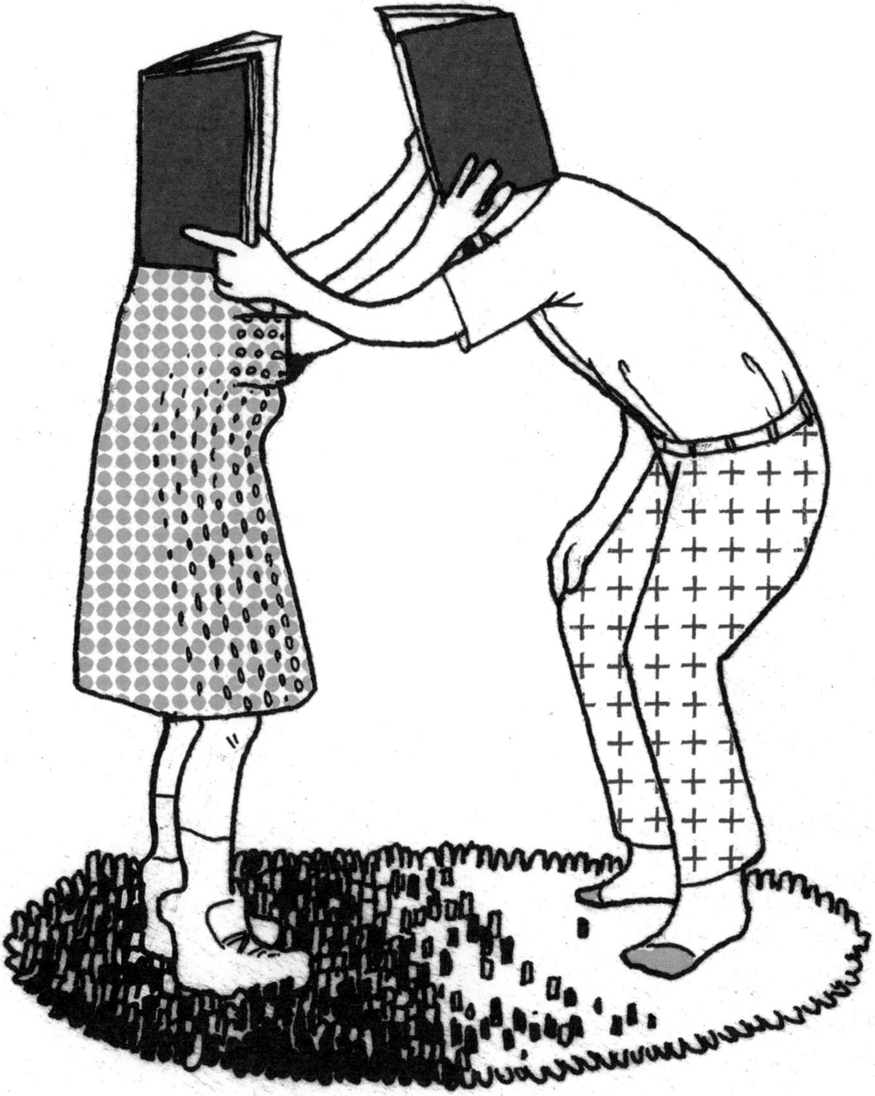

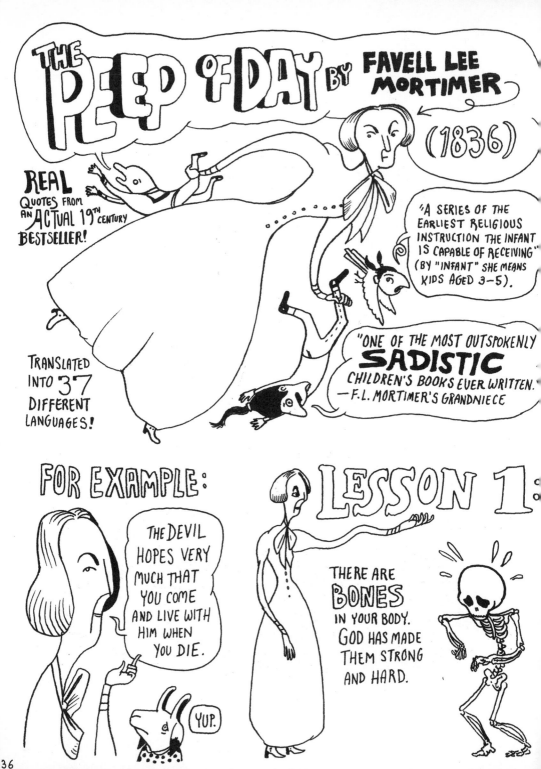

THE PEEP OF DAY BY FAVELL LEE MORTIMER (1836)

REAL QUOTES FROM AN ACTUAL 19TH CENTURY BESTSELLER!

"A SERIES OF THE EARLIEST RELIGIOUS INSTRUCTION THE INFANT IS CAPABLE OF RECEIVING" (BY "INFANT" SHE MEANS KIDS AGED 3-5).

"ONE OF THE MOST OUTSPOKENLY SADISTIC CHILDREN'S BOOKS EVER WRITTEN. —F.L. MORTIMER'S GRANDNIECE

TRANSLATED INTO 37 DIFFERENT LANGUAGES!

FOR EXAMPLE:

THE DEVIL HOPES VERY MUCH THAT YOU COME AND LIVE WITH HIM WHEN YOU DIE.

YUP.

LESSON 1:

THERE ARE BONES IN YOUR BODY. GOD HAS MADE THEM STRONG AND HARD.

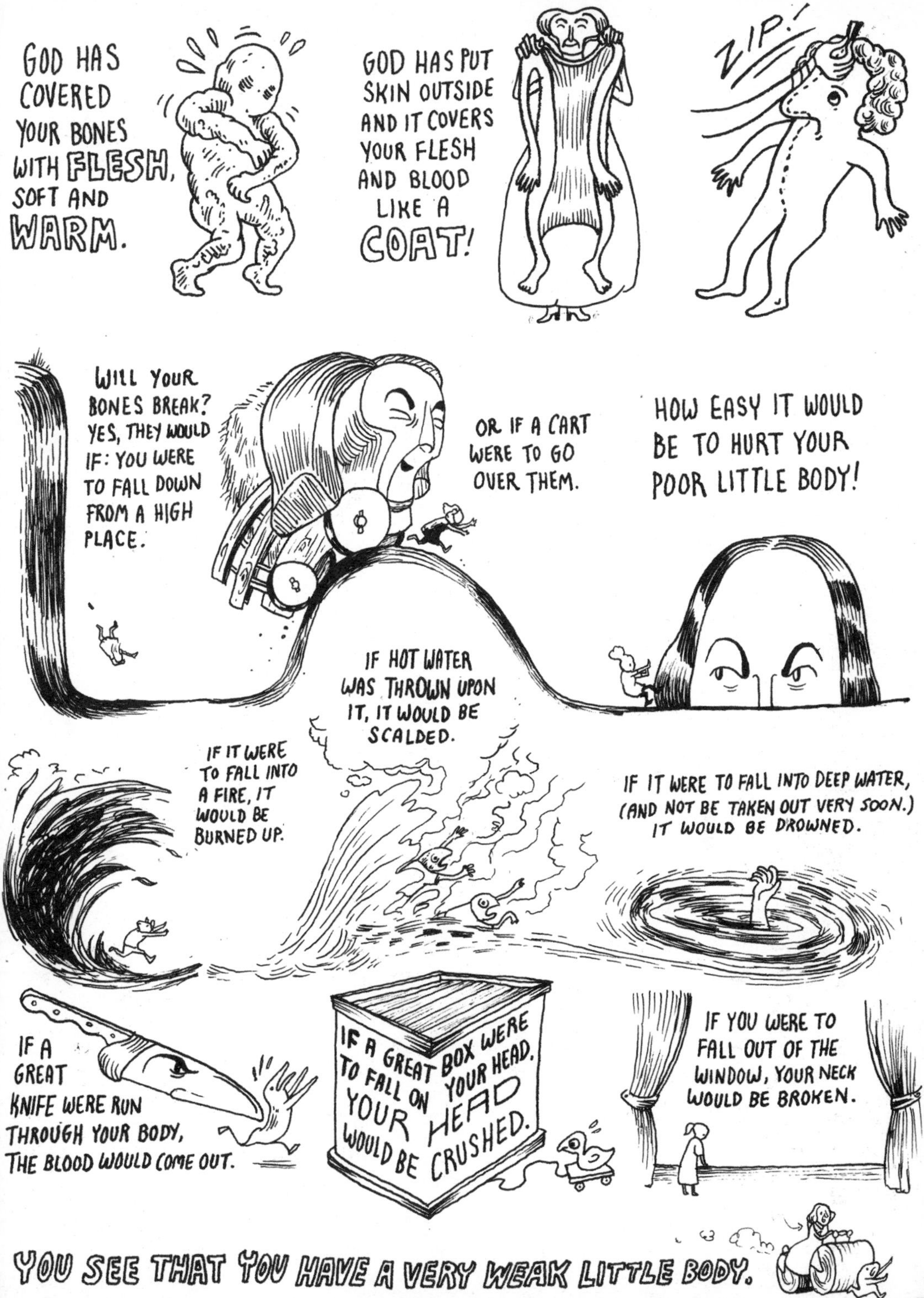
GOD HAS COVERED YOUR BONES WITH FLESH, SOFT AND WARM.
GOD HAS PUT SKIN OUTSIDE AND IT COVERS YOUR FLESH AND BLOOD LIKE A COAT!
ZIP!
WILL YOUR BONES BREAK? YES, THEY WOULD IF: YOU WERE TO FALL DOWN FROM A HIGH PLACE.
OR IF A CART WERE TO GO OVER THEM.
HOW EASY IT WOULD BE TO HURT YOUR POOR LITTLE BODY!
IF HOT WATER WAS THROWN UPON IT, IT WOULD BE SCALDED.
IF IT WERE TO FALL INTO A FIRE, IT WOULD BE BURNED UP.
IF IT WERE TO FALL INTO DEEP WATER, (AND NOT BE TAKEN OUT VERY SOON.) IT WOULD BE DROWNED.
IF A GREAT KNIFE WERE RUN THROUGH YOUR BODY, THE BLOOD WOULD COME OUT.
IF A GREAT BOX WERE TO FALL ON YOUR HEAD, YOUR HEAD WOULD BE CRUSHED.
IF YOU WERE TO FALL OUT OF THE WINDOW, YOUR NECK WOULD BE BROKEN.
YOU SEE THAT YOU HAVE A VERY WEAK LITTLE BODY.

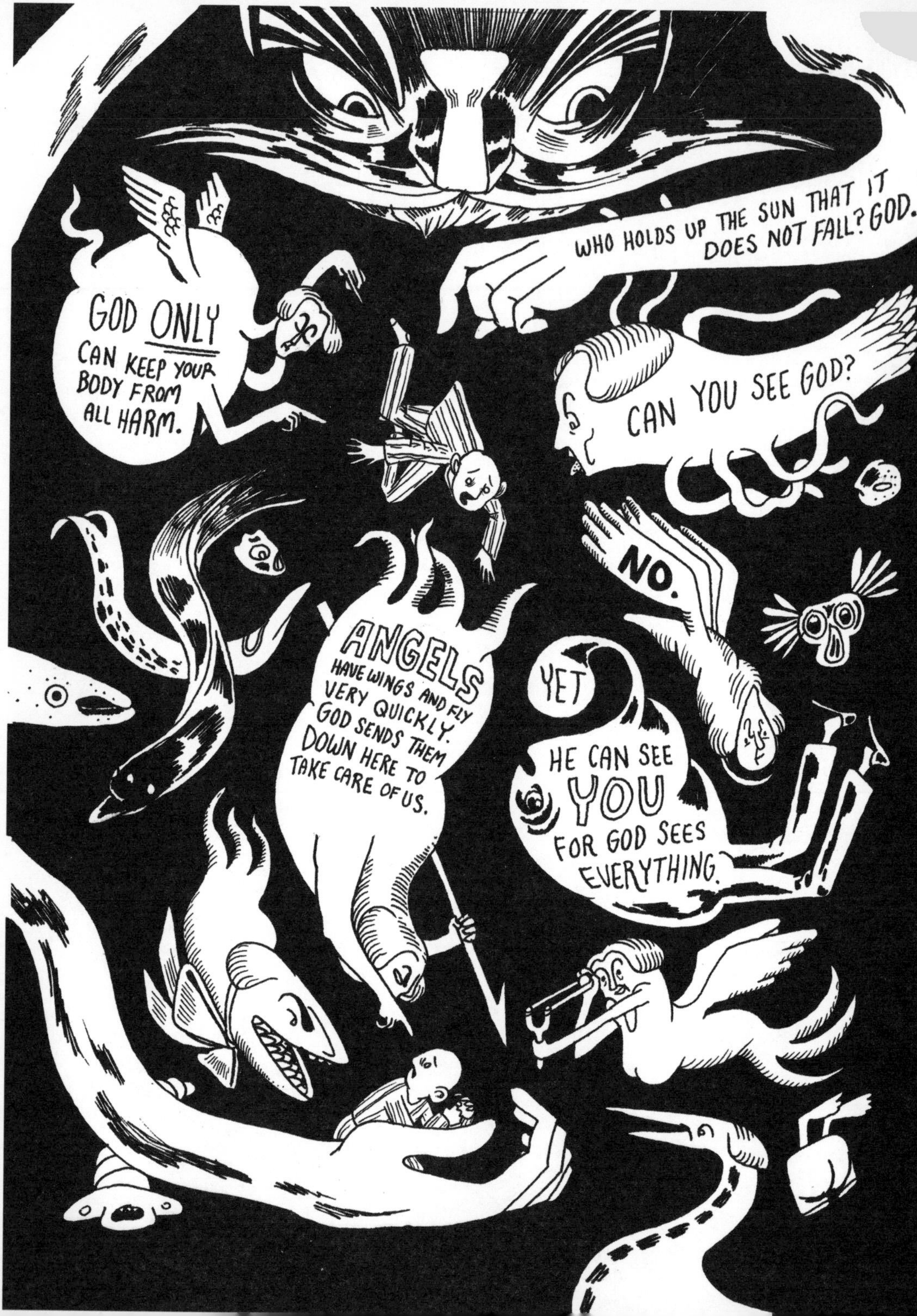
WHO HOLDS UP THE SUN THAT IT DOES NOT FALL? GOD.
GOD ONLY CAN KEEP YOUR BODY FROM ALL HARM.
CAN YOU SEE GOD?
NO.
ANGELS HAVE WINGS AND FLY VERY QUICKLY. GOD SENDS THEM DOWN HERE TO TAKE CARE OF US.
YET
HE CAN SEE YOU FOR GOD SEES EVERYTHING.

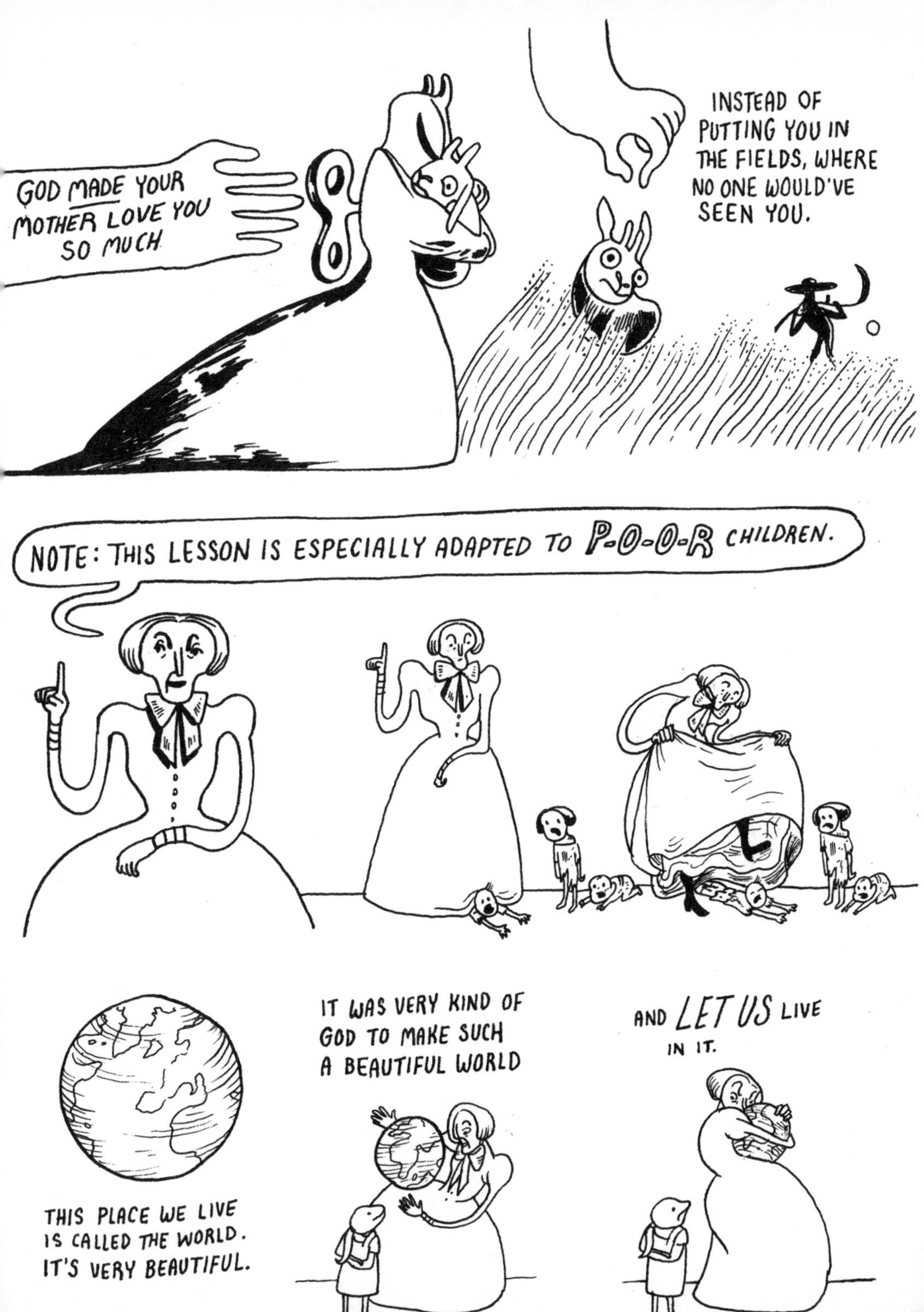
GOD MADE YOUR MOTHER LOVE YOU SO MUCH
INSTEAD OF PUTTING YOU IN THE FIELDS, WHERE NO ONE WOULD'VE SEEN YOU.
NOTE: THIS LESSON IS ESPECIALLY ADAPTED TO P-O-O-R CHILDREN.
THIS PLACE WE LIVE IS CALLED THE WORLD. IT'S VERY BEAUTIFUL.
IT WAS VERY KIND OF GOD TO MAKE SUCH A BEAUTIFUL WORLD
AND LET US LIVE IN IT.

THE BEST OF PEEP OF DAY:

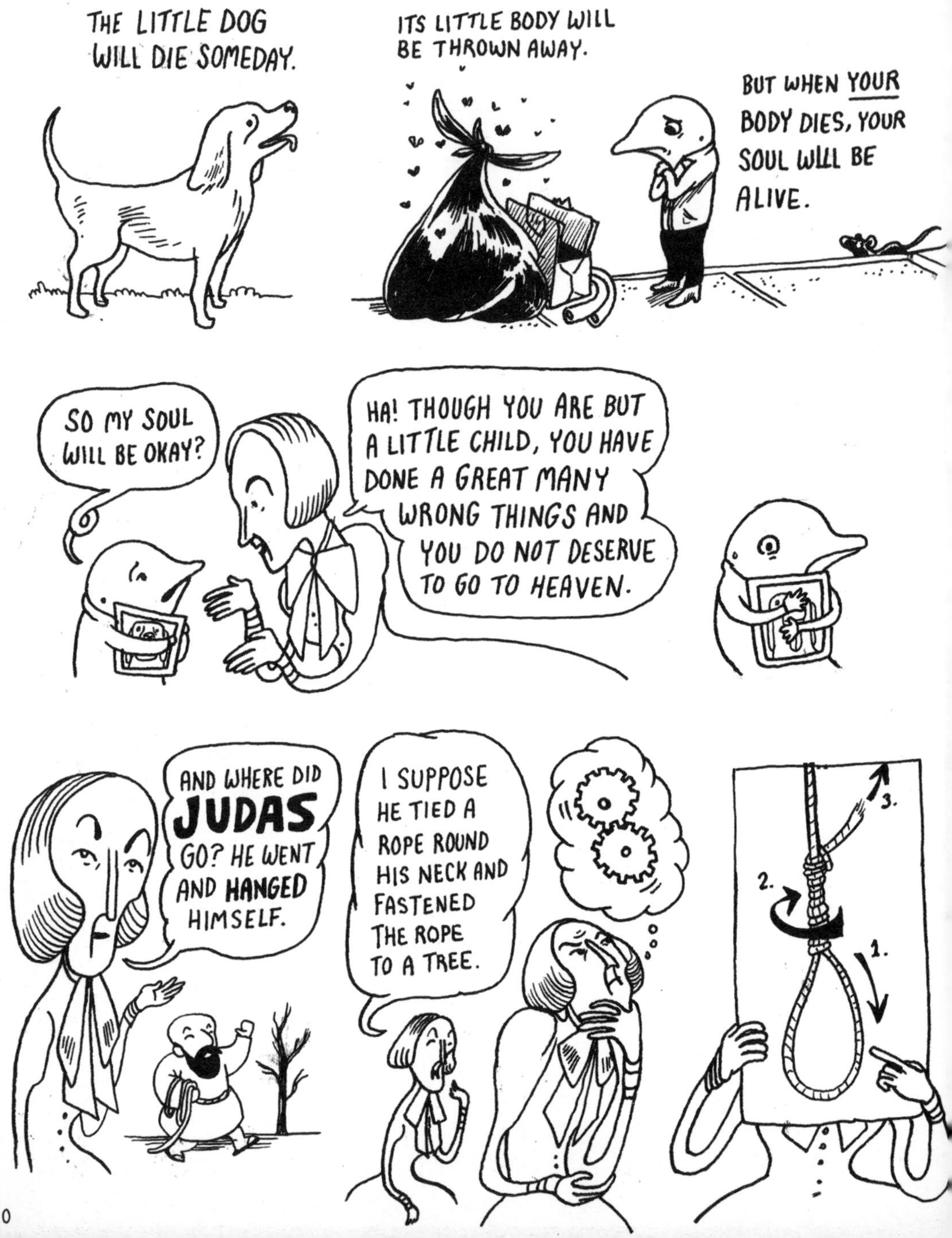

THE LITTLE DOG WILL DIE SOMEDAY.
ITS LITTLE BODY WILL BE THROWN AWAY.
BUT WHEN YOUR BODY DIES, YOUR SOUL WILL BE ALIVE.
SO MY SOUL WILL BE OKAY?
HA! THOUGH YOU ARE BUT A LITTLE CHILD, YOU HAVE DONE A GREAT MANY WRONG THINGS AND YOU DO NOT DESERVE TO GO TO HEAVEN.
AND WHERE DID JUDAS GO? HE WENT AND HANGED HIMSELF.
I SUPPOSE HE TIED A ROPE ROUND HIS NECK AND FASTENED THE ROPE TO A TREE.
1.
2.
3.

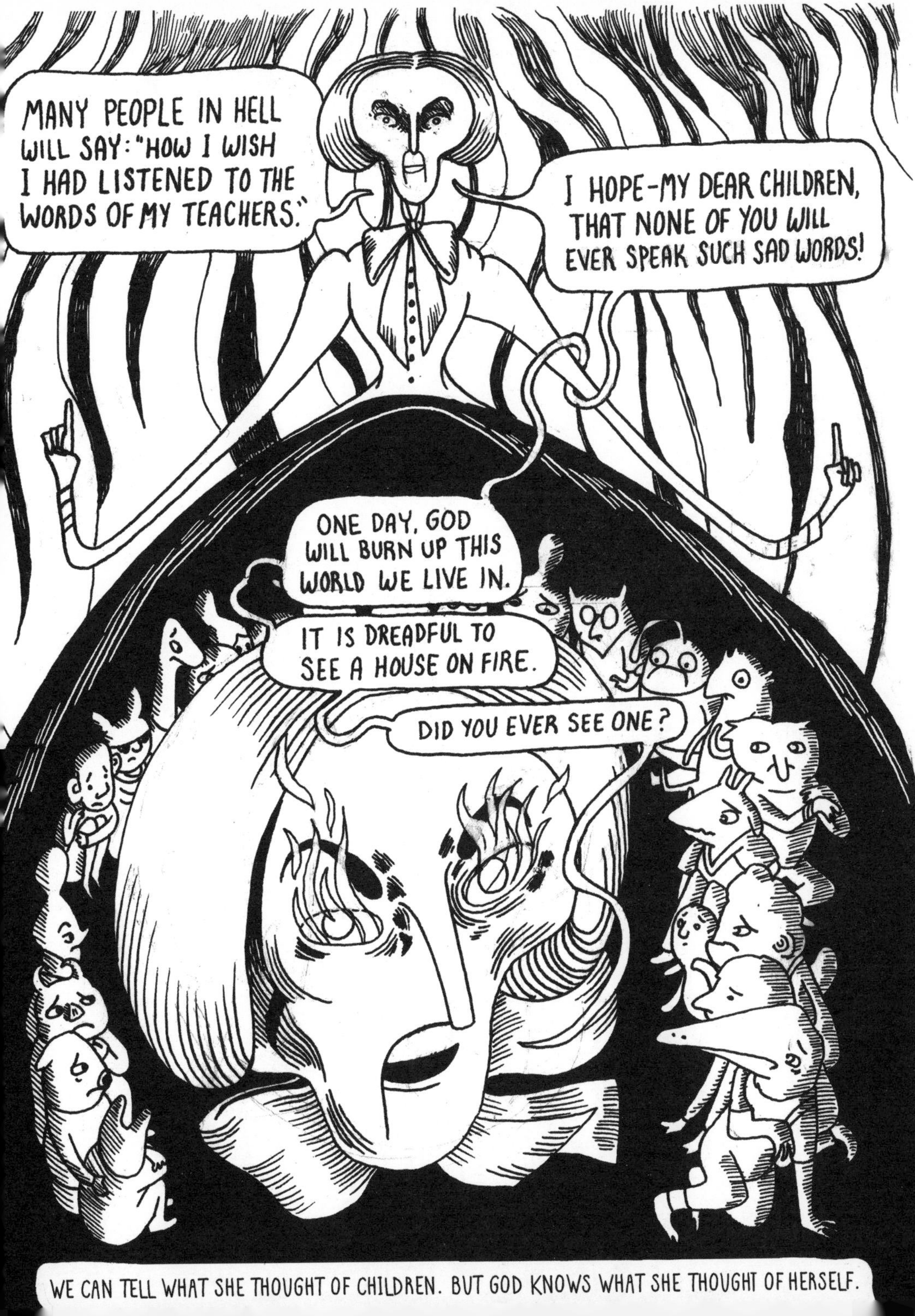
MANY PEOPLE IN HELL WILL SAY: "HOW I WISH I HAD LISTENED TO THE WORDS OF MY TEACHERS."
I HOPE-MY DEAR CHILDREN, THAT NONE OF YOU WILL EVER SPEAK SUCH SAD WORDS!
ONE DAY, GOD WILL BURN UP THIS WORLD WE LIVE IN.
IT IS DREADFUL TO SEE A HOUSE ON FIRE.
DID YOU EVER SEE ONE?
WE CAN TELL WHAT SHE THOUGHT OF CHILDREN. BUT GOD KNOWS WHAT SHE THOUGHT OF HERSELF.

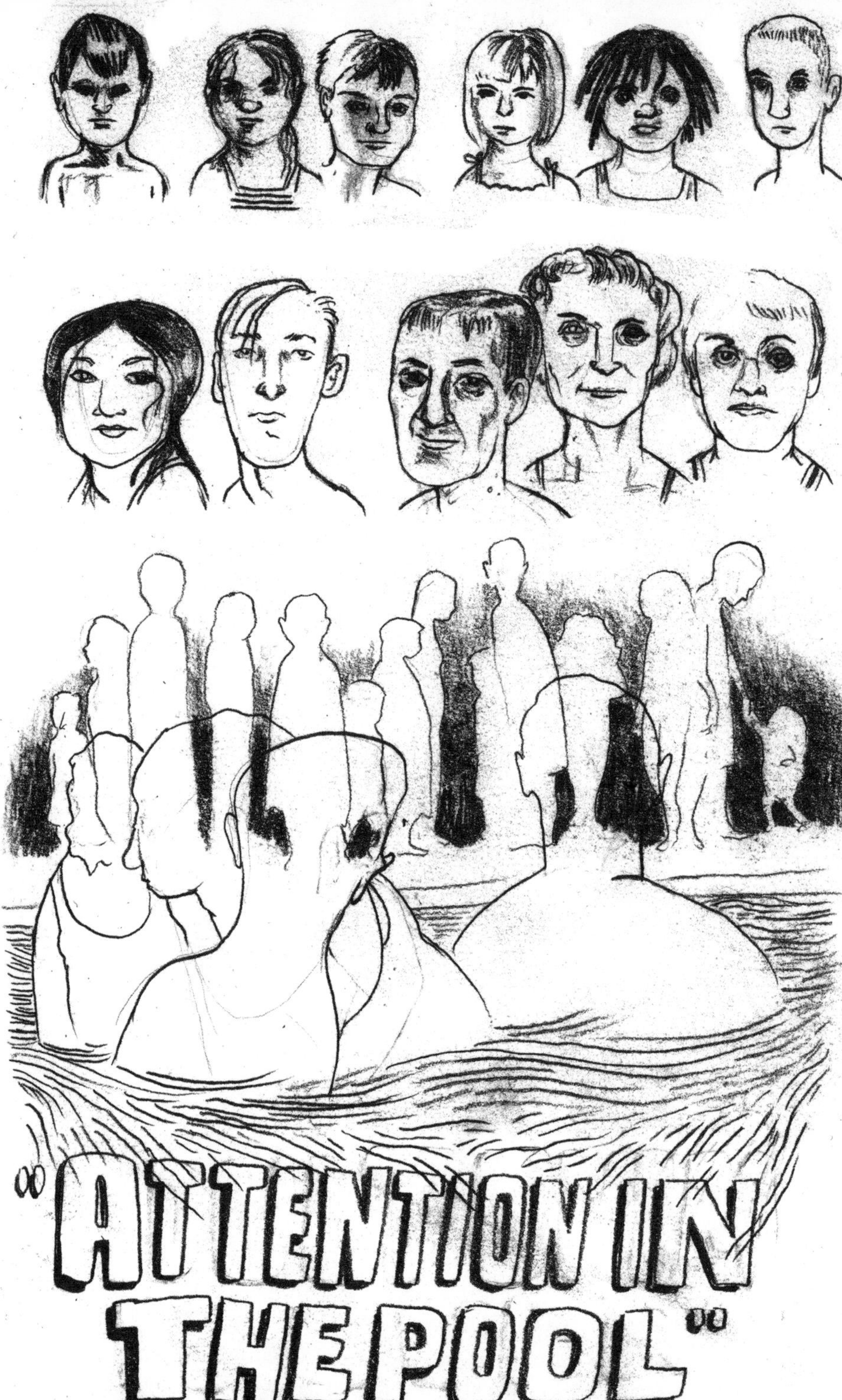
"ATTENTION IN THE POOL"

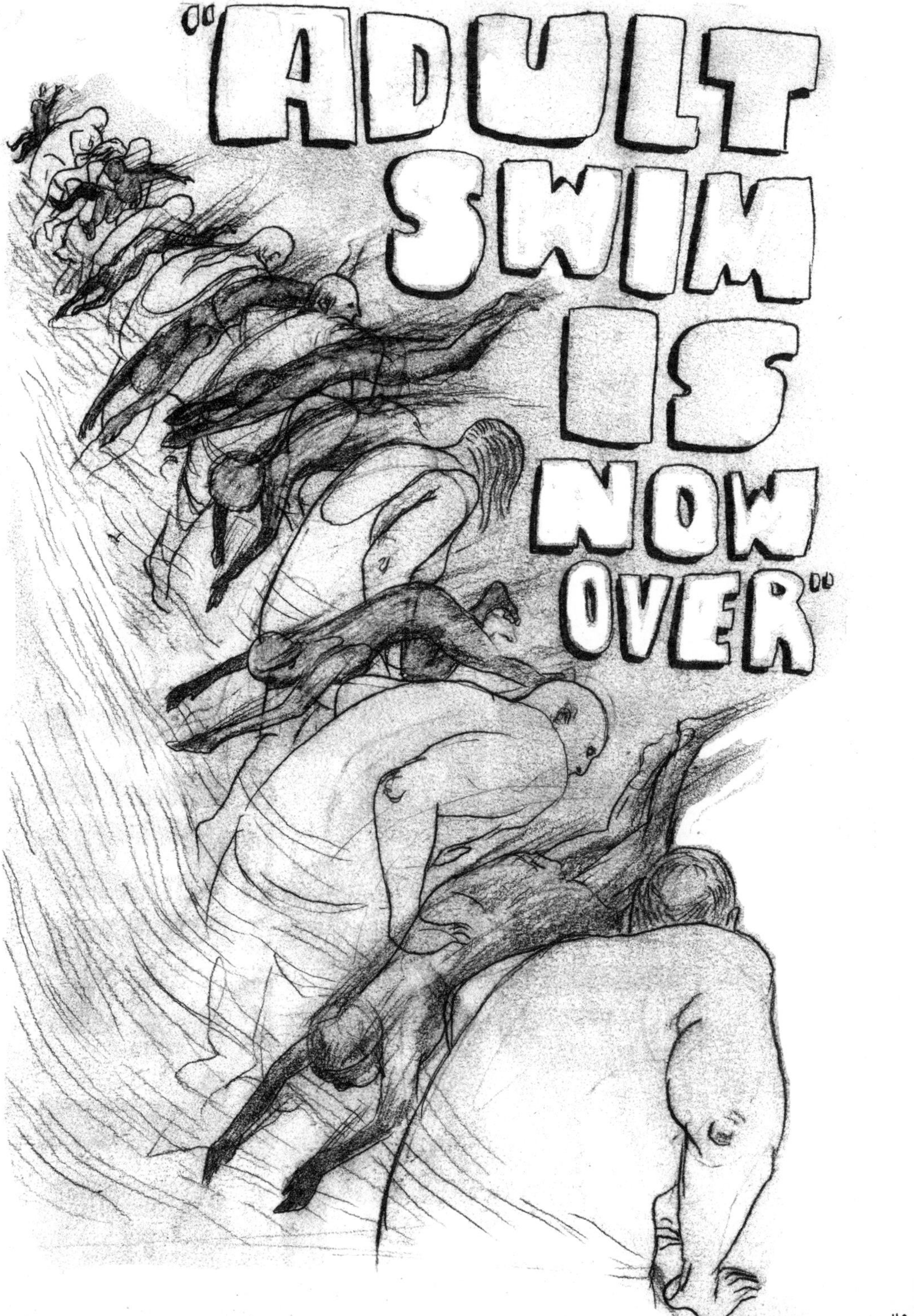
"ADULT
SWIM
IS
NOW
OVER"

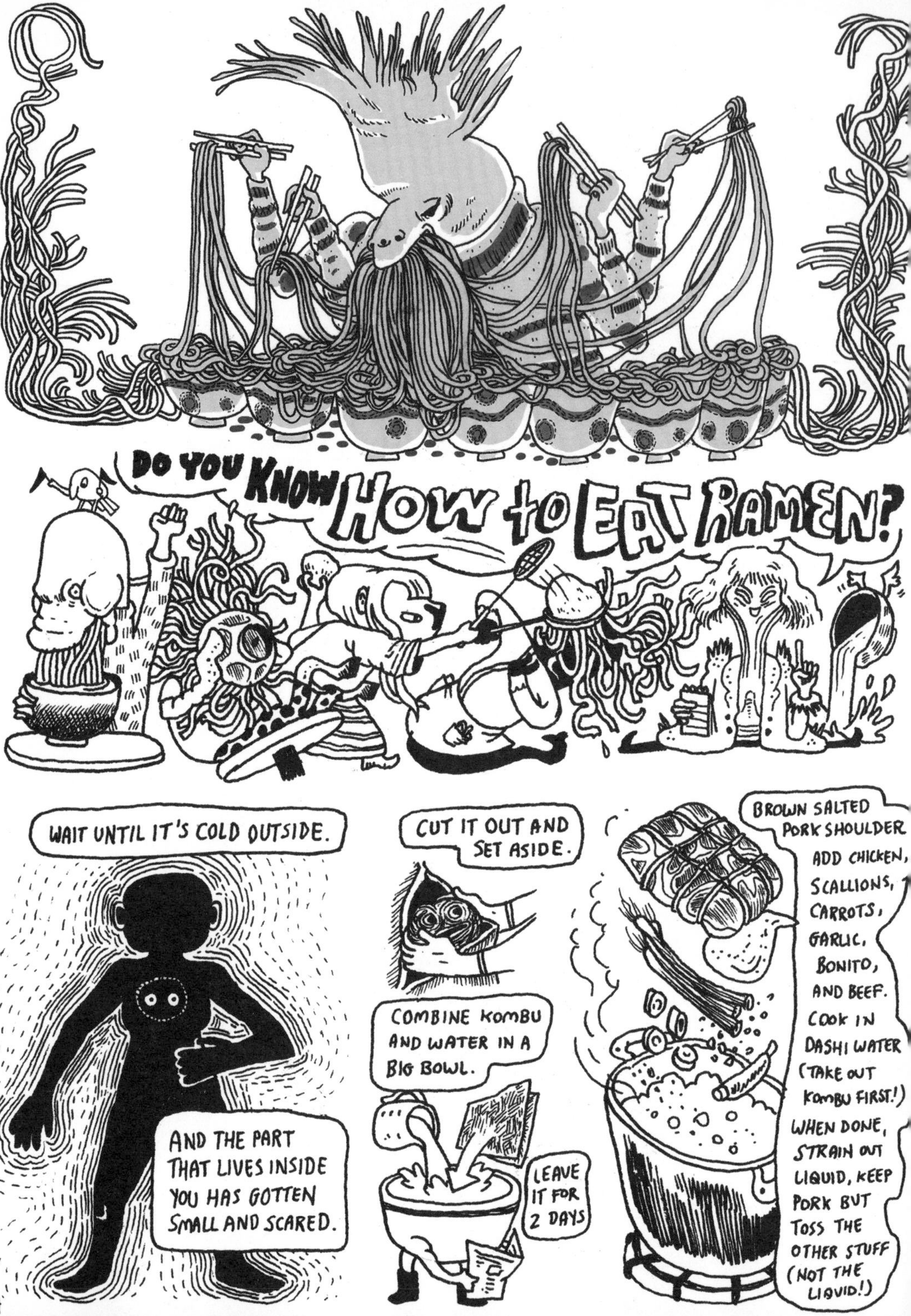
DO YOU KNOW HOW to EAT RAMEN?
WAIT UNTIL IT'S COLD OUTSIDE.
AND THE PART THAT LIVES INSIDE YOU HAS GOTTEN SMALL AND SCARED.
CUT IT OUT AND SET ASIDE.
COMBINE KOMBU AND WATER IN A BIG BOWL.
LEAVE IT FOR 2 DAYS
BROWN SALTED PORK SHOULDER
ADD CHICKEN, SCALLIONS, CARROTS, GARLIC, BONITO, AND BEEF.
COOK IN DASHI WATER (TAKE OUT KOMBU FIRST!)
WHEN DONE, STRAIN OUT LIQUID, KEEP PORK BUT TOSS THE OTHER STUFF (NOT THE LIQUID!)

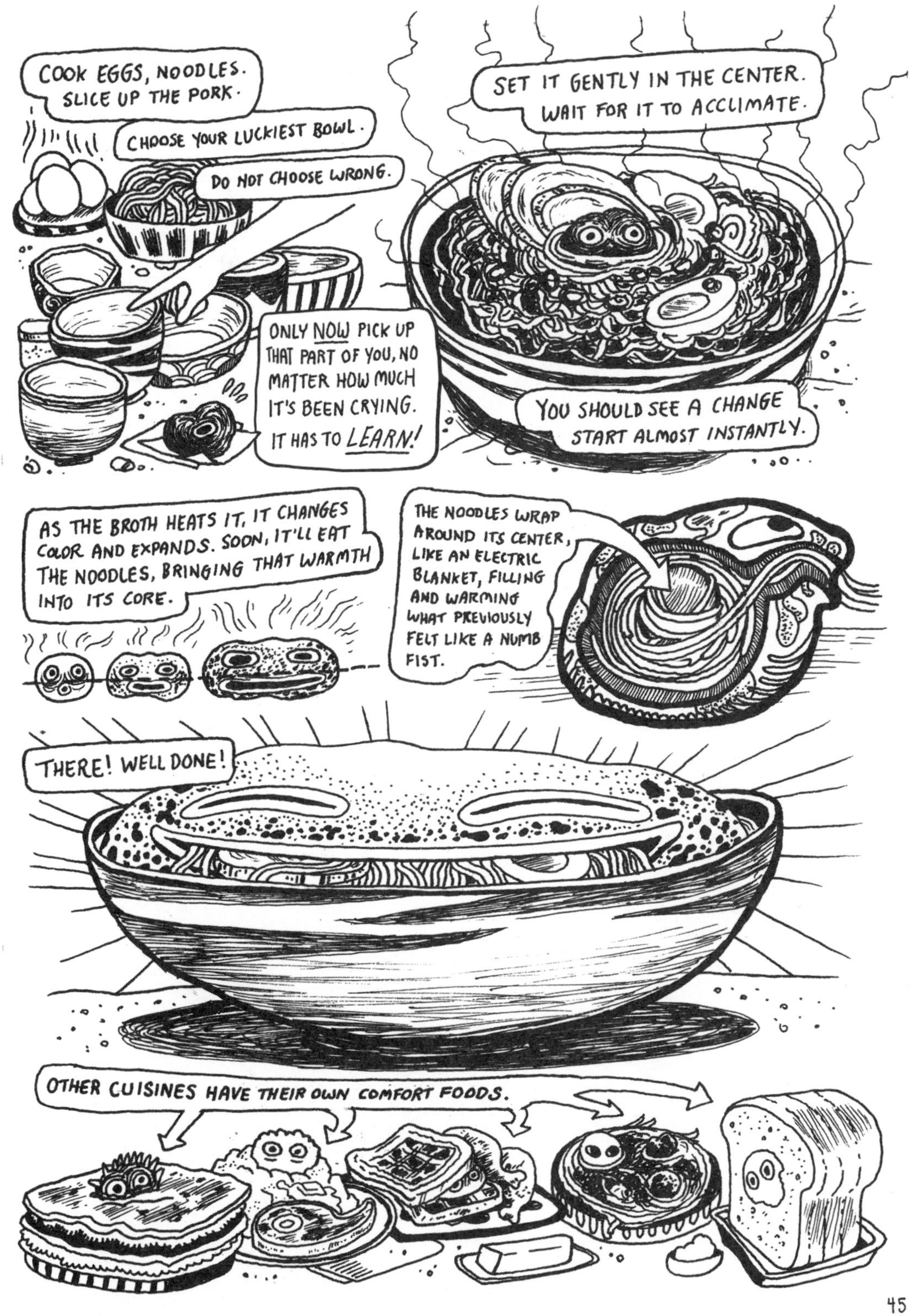

COOK EGGS, NOODLES. SLICE UP THE PORK.
CHOOSE YOUR LUCKIEST BOWL.
DO NOT CHOOSE WRONG.
ONLY NOW PICK UP THAT PART OF YOU, NO MATTER HOW MUCH IT'S BEEN CRYING. IT HAS TO LEARN!
SET IT GENTLY IN THE CENTER. WAIT FOR IT TO ACCLIMATE.
YOU SHOULD SEE A CHANGE START ALMOST INSTANTLY.
AS THE BROTH HEATS IT, IT CHANGES COLOR AND EXPANDS. SOON, IT'LL EAT THE NOODLES, BRINGING THAT WARMTH INTO ITS CORE.
THE NOODLES WRAP AROUND ITS CENTER, LIKE AN ELECTRIC BLANKET, FILLING AND WARMING WHAT PREVIOUSLY FELT LIKE A NUMB FIST.
THERE! WELL DONE!
OTHER CUISINES HAVE THEIR OWN COMFORT FOODS.

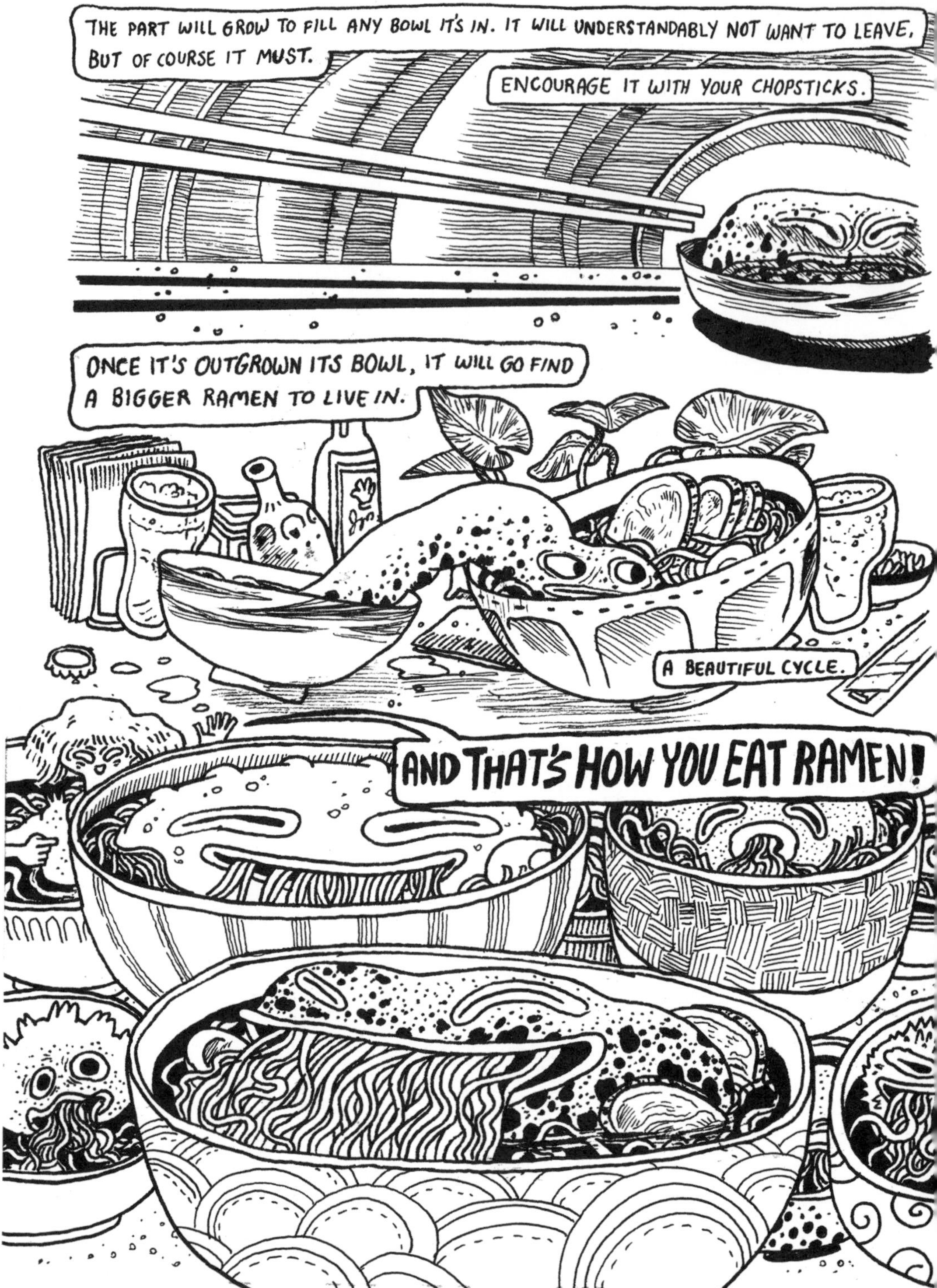
THE PART WILL GROW TO FILL ANY BOWL IT'S IN. IT WILL UNDERSTANDABLY NOT WANT TO LEAVE, BUT OF COURSE IT MUST.
ENCOURAGE IT WITH YOUR CHOPSTICKS.
ONCE IT'S OUTGROWN ITS BOWL, IT WILL GO FIND A BIGGER RAMEN TO LIVE IN.
A BEAUTIFUL CYCLE.
AND THAT'S HOW YOU EAT RAMEN!

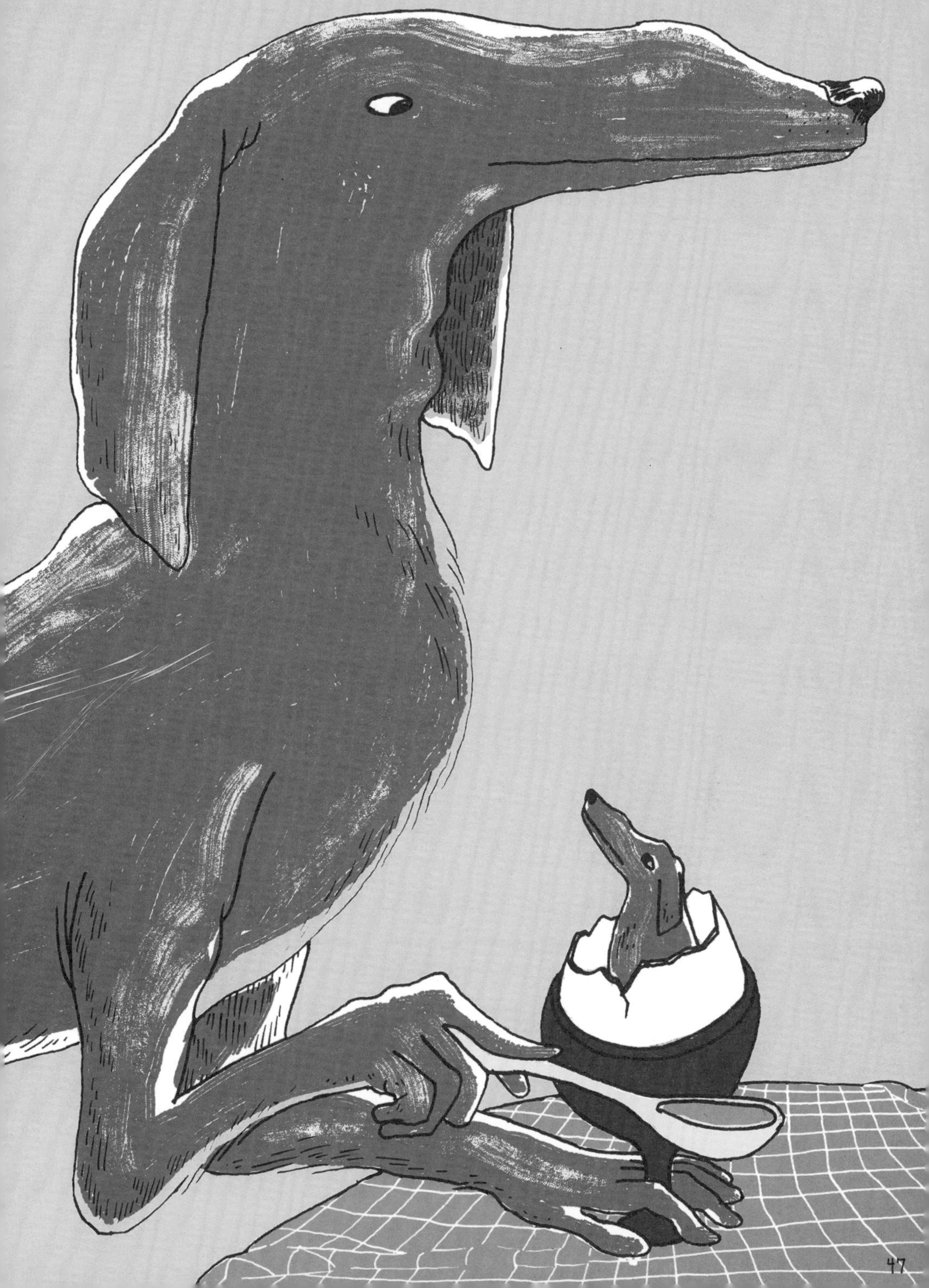

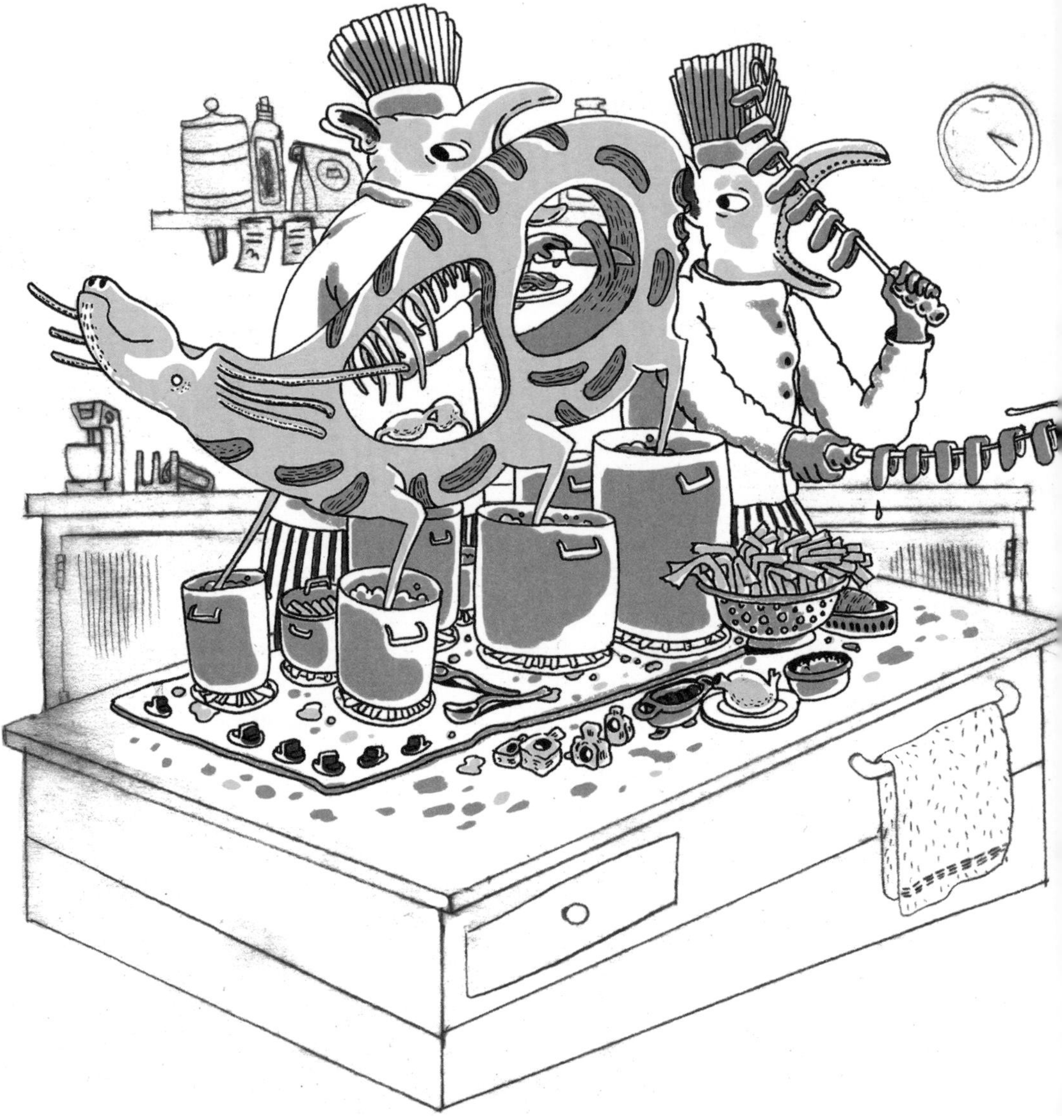

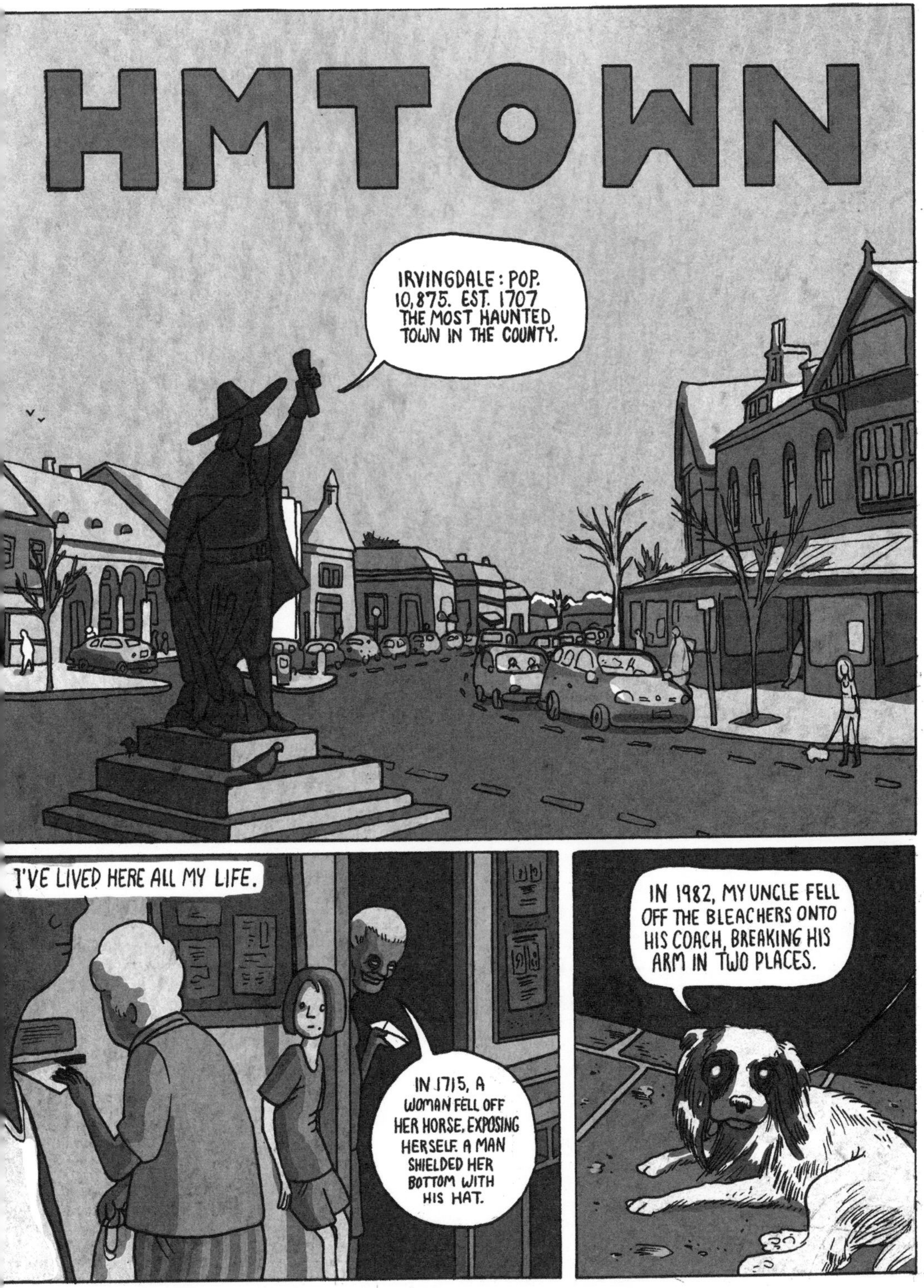
HMTOWN
IRVINGDALE: POP. 10,875. EST. 1707 THE MOST HAUNTED TOWN IN THE COUNTY.
I'VE LIVED HERE ALL MY LIFE.
IN 1715, A WOMAN FELL OFF HER HORSE, EXPOSING HERSELF. A MAN SHIELDED HER BOTTOM WITH HIS HAT.
IN 1982, MY UNCLE FELL OFF THE BLEACHERS ONTO HIS COACH, BREAKING HIS ARM IN TWO PLACES.

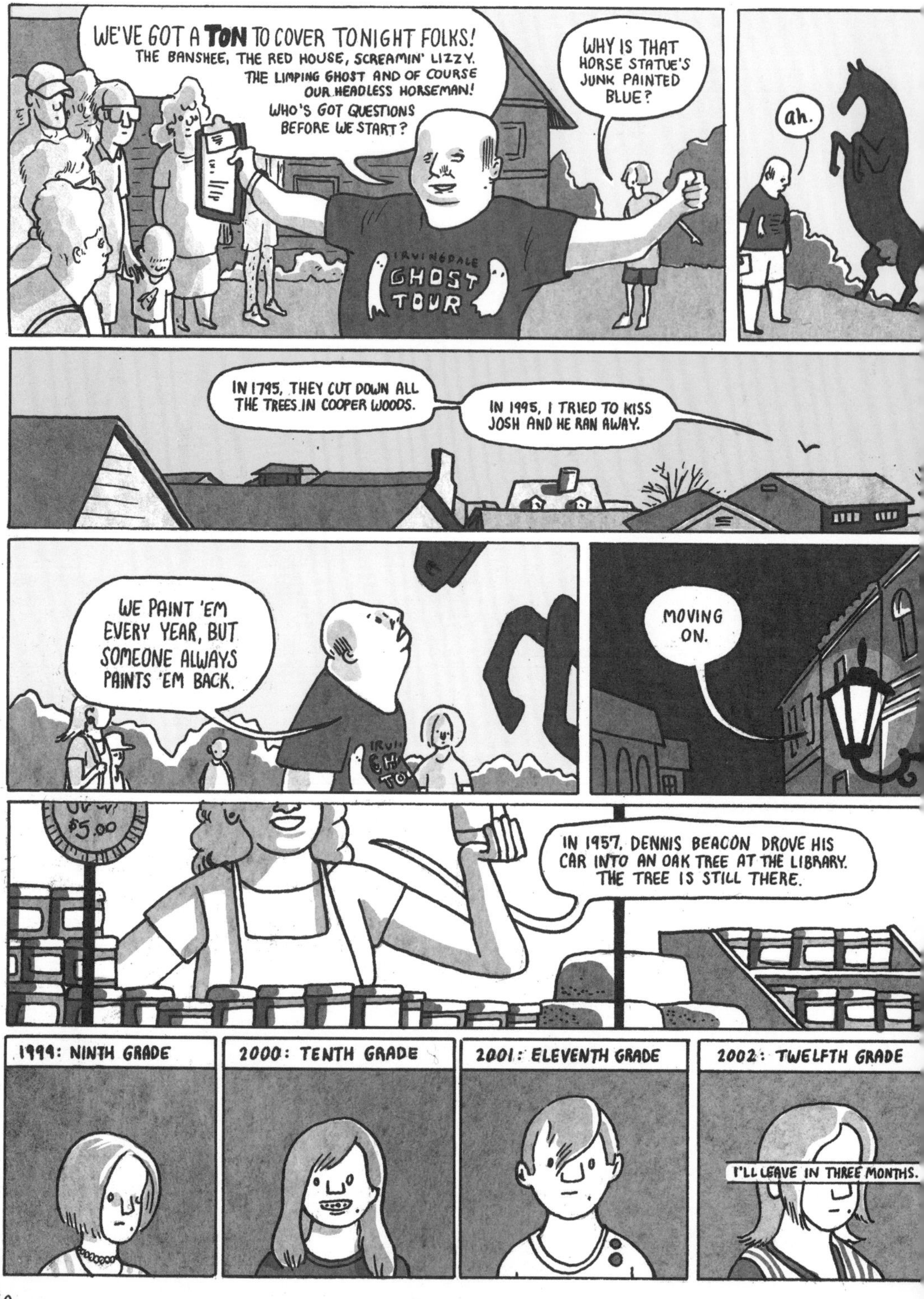
WE'VE GOT A TON TO COVER TONIGHT FOLKS!
THE BANSHEE, THE RED HOUSE, SCREAMIN' LIZZY. THE LIMPING GHOST AND OF COURSE OUR HEADLESS HORSEMAN!
WHO'S GOT QUESTIONS BEFORE WE START?
IRVINGDALE GHOST TOUR
WHY IS THAT HORSE STATUE'S JUNK PAINTED BLUE?
ah.
IN 1795, THEY CUT DOWN ALL THE TREES IN COOPER WOODS.
IN 1995, I TRIED TO KISS JOSH AND HE RAN AWAY.
WE PAINT 'EM EVERY YEAR, BUT SOMEONE ALWAYS PAINTS 'EM BACK.
MOVING ON.
$5.00
IN 1957, DENNIS BEACON DROVE HIS CAR INTO AN OAK TREE AT THE LIBRARY. THE TREE IS STILL THERE.
1999: NINTH GRADE
2000: TENTH GRADE
2001: ELEVENTH GRADE
2002: TWELFTH GRADE
I'LL LEAVE IN THREE MONTHS.

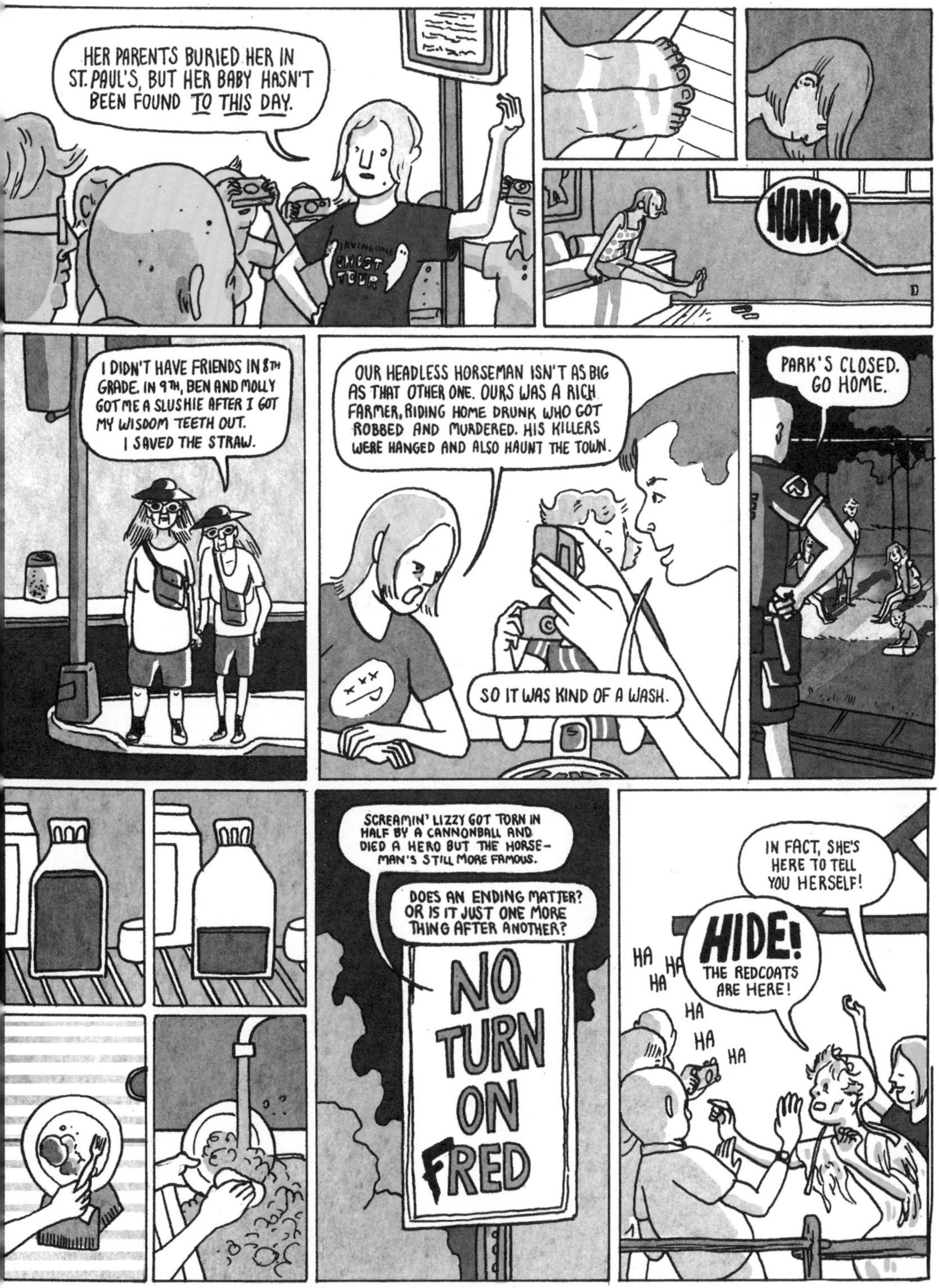
HER PARENTS BURIED HER IN ST. PAUL'S, BUT HER BABY HASN'T BEEN FOUND TO THIS DAY.
IRVINGDALE GHOST TOUR
HONK
I DIDN'T HAVE FRIENDS IN 8TH GRADE. IN 9TH, BEN AND MOLLY GOT ME A SLUSHIE AFTER I GOT MY WISDOM TEETH OUT. I SAVED THE STRAW.
OUR HEADLESS HORSEMAN ISN'T AS BIG AS THAT OTHER ONE. OURS WAS A RICH FARMER, RIDING HOME DRUNK WHO GOT ROBBED AND MURDERED. HIS KILLERS WERE HANGED AND ALSO HAUNT THE TOWN.
SO IT WAS KIND OF A WASH.
PARK'S CLOSED. GO HOME.
SCREAMIN' LIZZY GOT TORN IN HALF BY A CANNONBALL AND DIED A HERO BUT THE HORSE-MAN'S STILL MORE FAMOUS.
DOES AN ENDING MATTER? OR IS IT JUST ONE MORE THING AFTER ANOTHER?
NO TURN ON FRED
IN FACT, SHE'S HERE TO TELL YOU HERSELF!
HIDE! THE REDCOATS ARE HERE!
HA HA HA HA HA HA HA

HAS ANYONE EVER WASHED THIS COSTUME?

WELL, IT'S *SUPPOSED* TO SMELL LIKE SOMEONE DIED IN IT.

HA.HA.

IS IT TIME FOR THE GHOSTS TO GET BURRITOS YET?

MOLLY, YOU COMING?

NAH, RAY AND I ARE GONNA GO GET DONUTS.

IN 1843, A BEGGAR DROWNED IN A CREEK.

HE BECAME THE LIMPING GHOST. IN 1943, SUSAN'S GRANDPA WATCHED HIS HOUSE BURN DOWN. THEN, HE WALKED TO THE DINER FOR COFFEE.

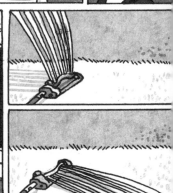

LIE DOWN, I DON'T SEE ANY CARS.

I TOLD MOM I WOULDN'T WANT TO RAISE KIDS HERE AND SHE GOT UPSET. YOU THINK YOU'LL EVER DO THAT?

NO ONE MOVES BACK HERE, THEY JUST VISIT.

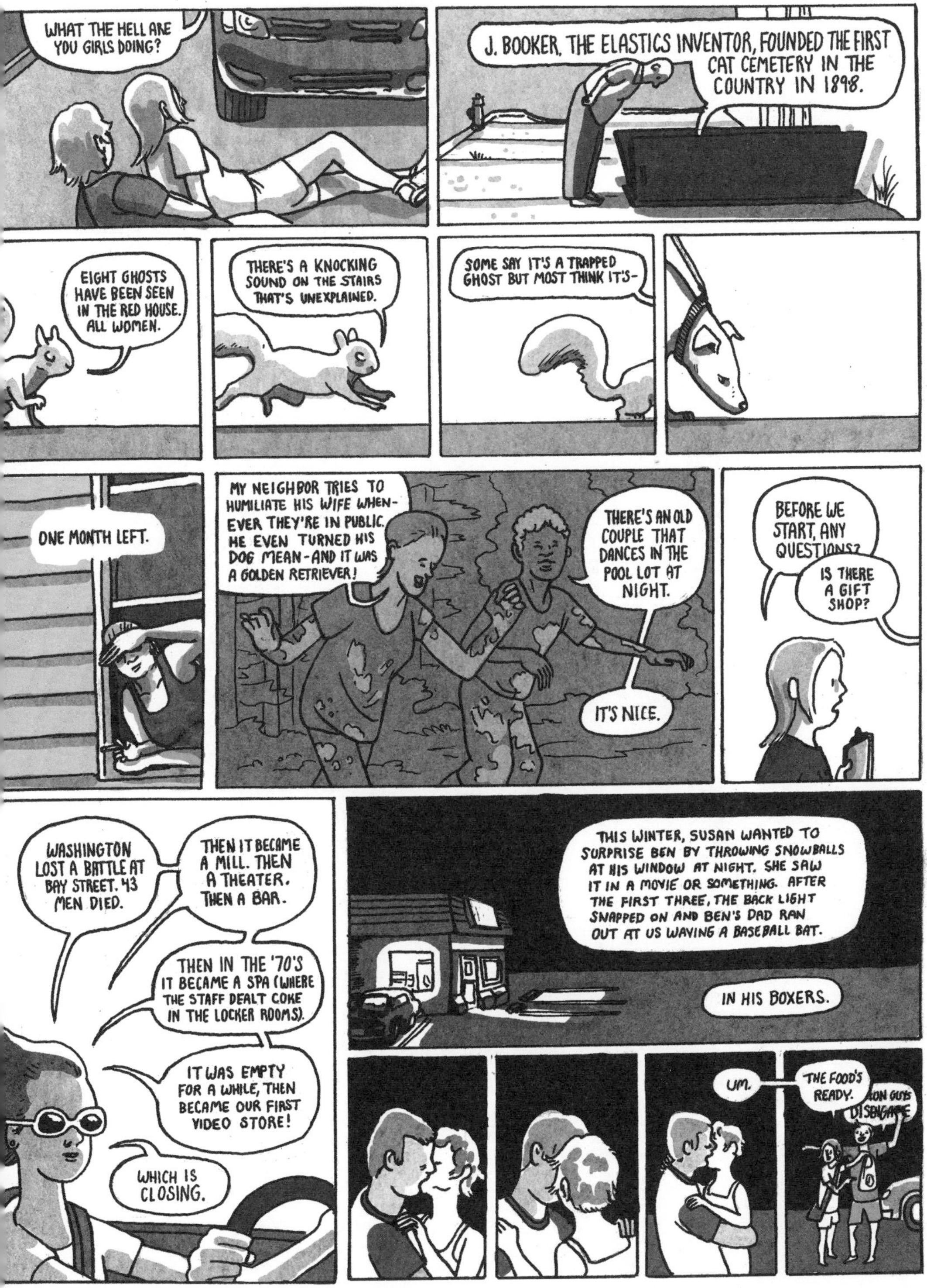

WHAT THE HELL ARE YOU GIRLS DOING?
J. BOOKER, THE ELASTICS INVENTOR, FOUNDED THE FIRST CAT CEMETERY IN THE COUNTRY IN 1898.
EIGHT GHOSTS HAVE BEEN SEEN IN THE RED HOUSE. ALL WOMEN.
THERE'S A KNOCKING SOUND ON THE STAIRS THAT'S UNEXPLAINED.
SOME SAY IT'S A TRAPPED GHOST BUT MOST THINK IT'S-
ONE MONTH LEFT.
MY NEIGHBOR TRIES TO HUMILIATE HIS WIFE WHEN-EVER THEY'RE IN PUBLIC. HE EVEN TURNED HIS DOG MEAN-AND IT WAS A GOLDEN RETRIEVER!
THERE'S AN OLD COUPLE THAT DANCES IN THE POOL LOT AT NIGHT.
IT'S NICE.
BEFORE WE START, ANY QUESTIONS?
IS THERE A GIFT SHOP?
WASHINGTON LOST A BATTLE AT BAY STREET. 43 MEN DIED.
THEN IT BECAME A MILL. THEN A THEATER. THEN A BAR.
THEN IN THE '70'S IT BECAME A SPA (WHERE THE STAFF DEALT COKE IN THE LOCKER ROOMS).
IT WAS EMPTY FOR A WHILE, THEN BECAME OUR FIRST VIDEO STORE!
WHICH IS CLOSING.
THIS WINTER, SUSAN WANTED TO SURPRISE BEN BY THROWING SNOWBALLS AT HIS WINDOW AT NIGHT. SHE SAW IT IN A MOVIE OR SOMETHING. AFTER THE FIRST THREE, THE BACK LIGHT SNAPPED ON AND BEN'S DAD RAN OUT AT US WAVING A BASEBALL BAT.
IN HIS BOXERS.
UM.
THE FOOD'S READY.

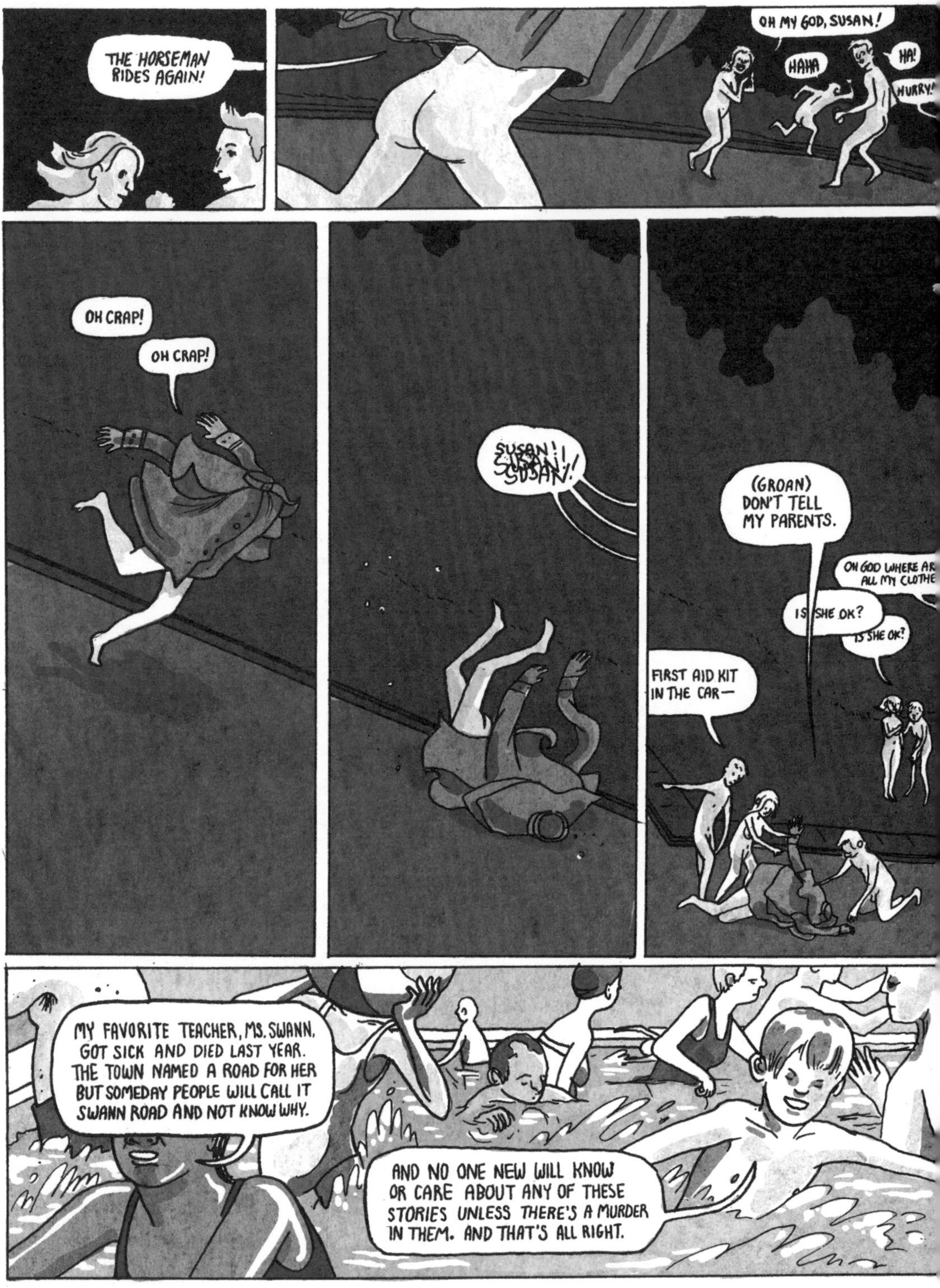

THE HORSEMAN RIDES AGAIN!
OH MY GOD, SUSAN!
HAHA
HA!
HURRY!
OH CRAP!
OH CRAP!
SUSAN! SUSAN! SUSAN!
(GROAN) DON'T TELL MY PARENTS.
OH GOD WHERE AR ALL MY CLOTHE
IS SHE OK?
IS SHE OK?
FIRST AID KIT IN THE CAR—
MY FAVORITE TEACHER, MS. SWANN, GOT SICK AND DIED LAST YEAR. THE TOWN NAMED A ROAD FOR HER BUT SOMEDAY PEOPLE WILL CALL IT SWANN ROAD AND NOT KNOW WHY.
AND NO ONE NEW WILL KNOW OR CARE ABOUT ANY OF THESE STORIES UNLESS THERE'S A MURDER IN THEM. AND THAT'S ALL RIGHT.

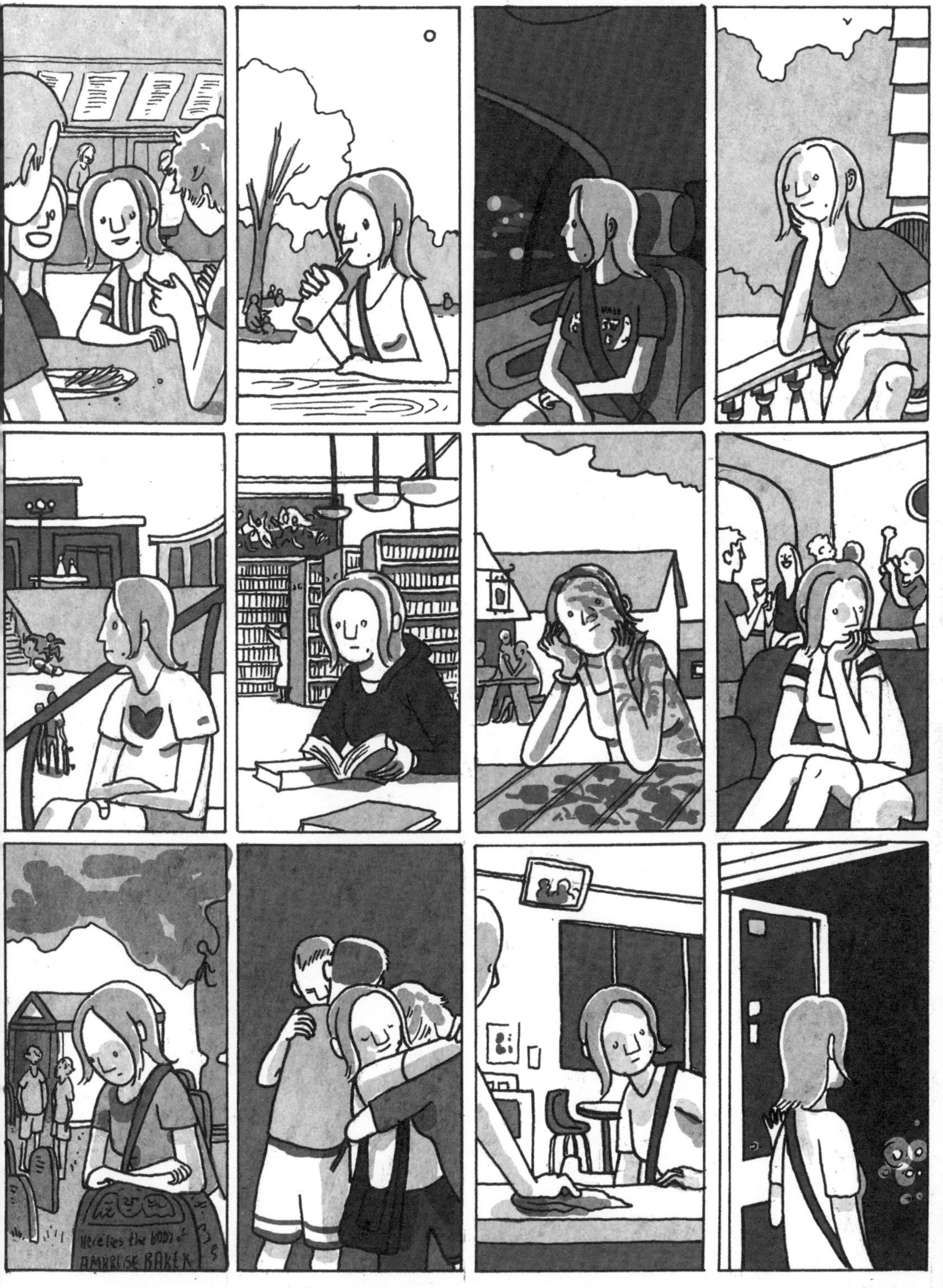
Here lies the BODY of
AMBROSE BAKER

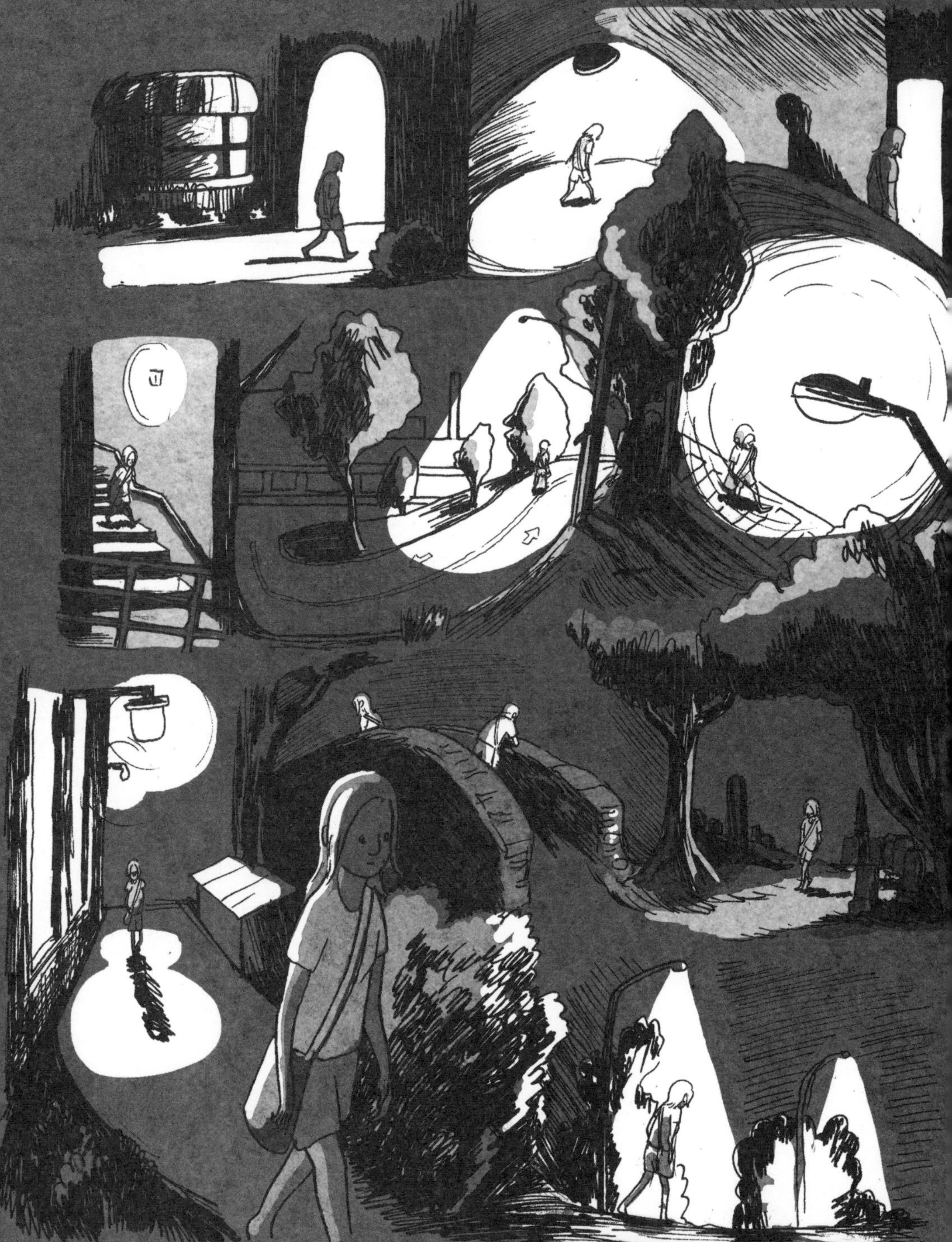

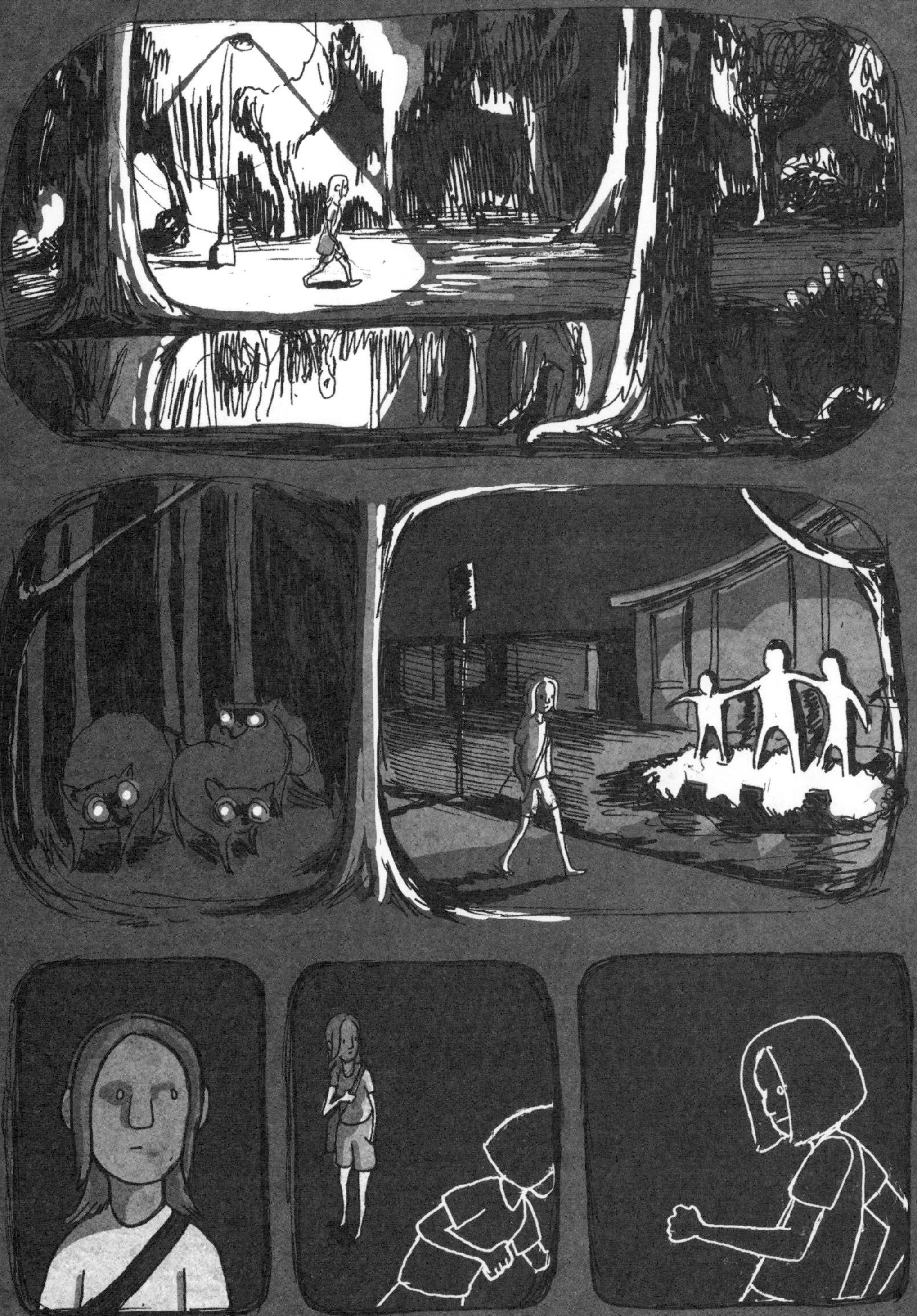

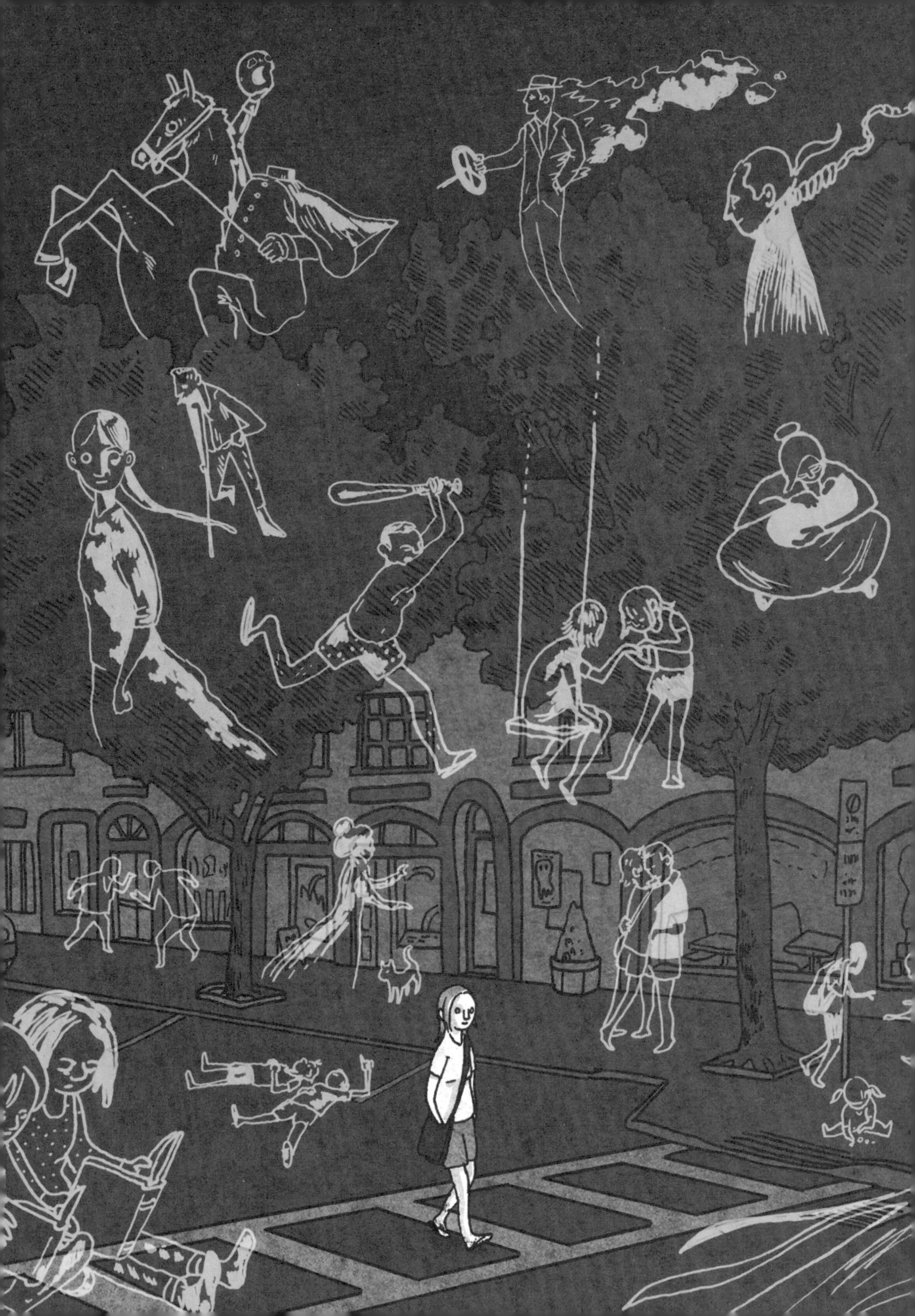

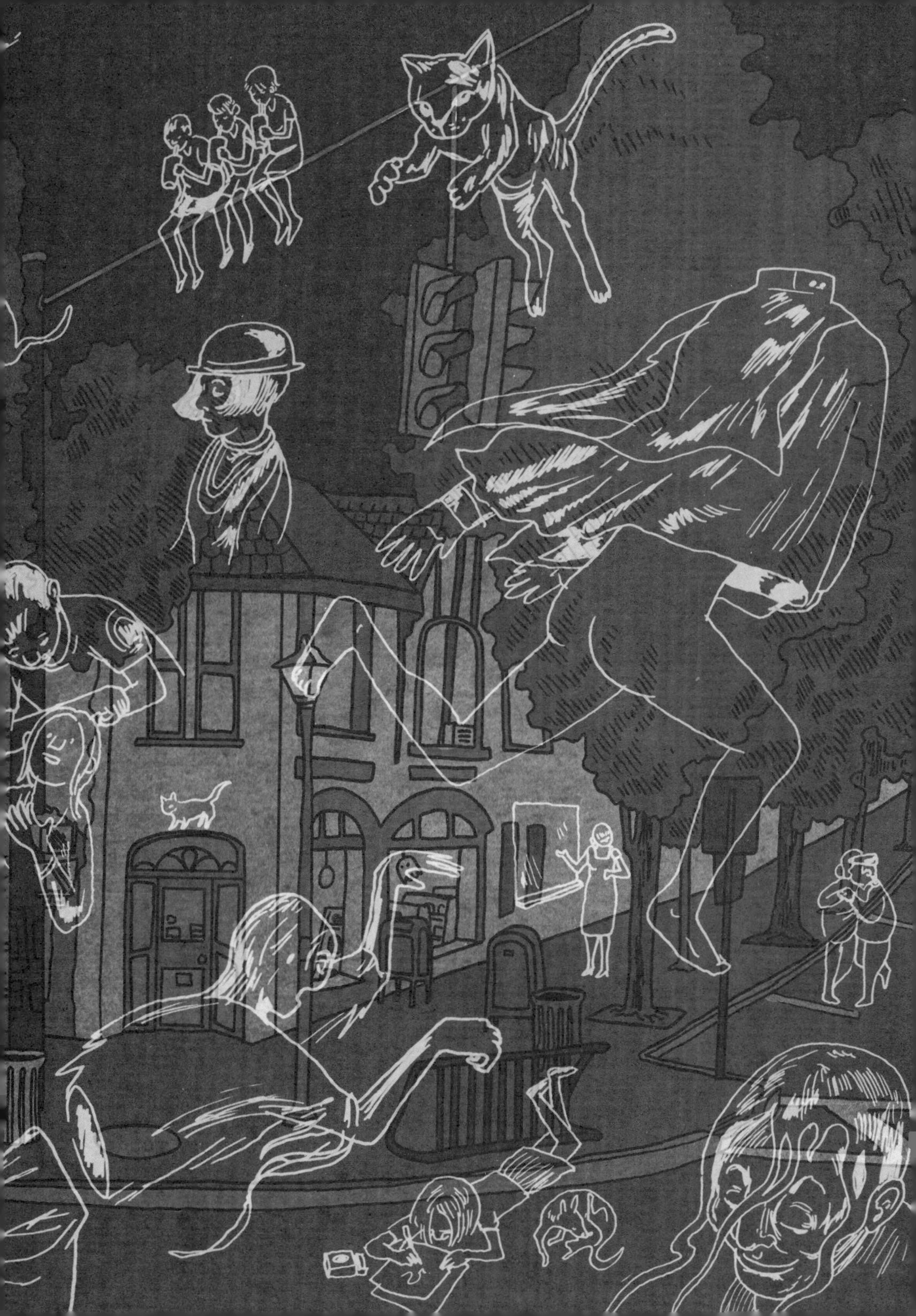

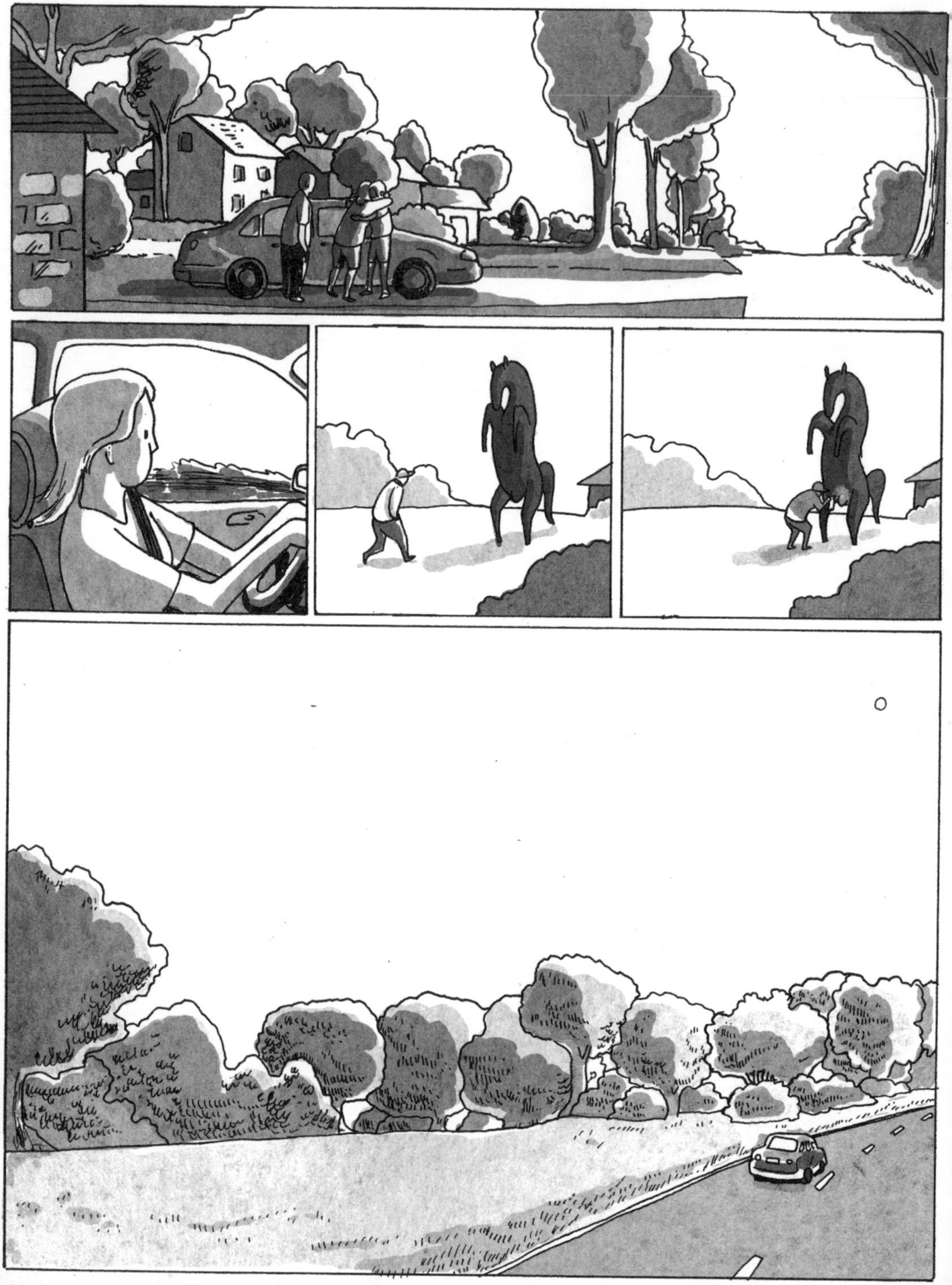